Living The Write Life:

Tips on making the most of your writing skills

Living The Write Life:

Tips on making the most of your writing skills

Traci M. Sanders

The author's intent in providing this book is to offer tutorial advice on topics related to the writing and publishing industry. Any book references or links, or name references, have been agreed upon by the original owners of this content.

Table of Contents

Introduction   7

General advice on authorship   9

TIP 324: 10 ways being an author is like being a parent   11

TIP 325: Grow a spine, grow your fan base   13

TIP 326: Are you a starving artist?   15

TIP 327: Sometimes you just have to say "no"!   18

TIP 328: Keeping up with the Joneses   20

TIP 329: Are you ready to write that?   22

TIP 330: Sharing your WIP (work in progress)   24

TIP 331: Are you a one-book wonder?   26

TIP 332: Writing dreams Vs. Writing goals   28

TIP 333: 25 qualities most serious writers have in common   32

TIP 334: 10 ways writing a list can keep you from feeling "listless"   35

TIP 335: Do you have a book in you?   37

TIP 336: All by myself   40

TIP 337: Living with non-writers   43

TIP 338: We're human before we're anything else   47

TIP 339: Answering questions about being an author   49

TIP 340: Retreat and recharge to write better   54

TIP 341: Learn to take a compliment   56

TIP 342: Overcoming procrastination   60

TIP 343: The company you keep… 64

TIP 344: Finding your voice as a writer 66

TIP 345: The write way to get through the holidays 69

TIP 346: Striking a balance 71

TIP 347: 11 ways to find inspiration for your writing 75

TIP 348: 21 items to have in your writing workspace 78

TIP 349: Writing challenges or excuses? 82

TIP 350: Facing your fears 86

TIP 351: 7 great stretches for a writer 90

TIP 352: Tidbits of wisdom from experienced authors 94

Bonus resources to help you on your journey through authorship! 99

TIP 353: My 3 go-to books on writing 101

TIP 354: Writers' grants and where to find them 103

TIP 355: Protecting your work 105

TIP 356: 15 Cool tools for authors 107

TIP 357: HTML codes to enhance your Amazon listings 112

TIP 358: What you can "write off" as an author 116

TIP 359: 8 ways to save money 119

TIP 360: 5 items an author should always have handy 122

TIP 361: A writer's 3 best friends 124

TIP 362: And the award goes to… 127

TIP 363: The "I'm blocked' jar 129

TIP 364: Sites that help hone your writing skills 131

TIP 365: Use your voice 133

FINAL TIP: 135

Introduction

In 2016, I hosted a daily segment on my blog *A Word With Traci* (www.awordwithtraci.com) in which I offered tips on various aspects of the publishing industry. Most of these tips were aimed at Indie authors, but some applied to traditionally published authors as well.

The topics included writing, editing, publishing, and marketing.

Now, you can have all these tips in the palm of your hand, broken down into three easy-to-follow guides that cover specific stages of the publishing process:

Before You Publish (Volume I): Tips on grammar, writing, and editing

Beyond The Book (Volume II): Tips on publishing, marketing, and networking to build your brand

Living The Write Life (Volume III): Tips on making the most of your writing skills

Whether you have been in the publishing game for decades, or you are just getting started on this unpredictable-but-thrilling ride, you are sure to discover some new ideas in these books that will help you along on your writing journey.

***

This book offers tips on how to handle the day-to-day aspects of being an author, as well as how to capitalize on your writing talents.

It follows Volume II of this series, in which I offer tips on publishing, marketing, and networking.

So, dive in, bookmark the tips you like, and discard the ones that you don't need. I'm happy to answer any questions or address any topics you feel aren't covered in this series. You may email at tsanderpublishing@yaho.com.

Thank you for taking the time to read my books. I wish you much success in your own publishing endeavors!

General advice on authorship

TIP 324: 10 ways being an author is like being a parent

Parents love to show off their kids, don't they? And parents can become extremely defensive over their children. They nurture them, protect them, and then stand back and hope they find their way in the world.

Well, being an author is quite similar to being a parent, in several ways. If you don't believe me, check out any author's Facebook timeline. You'll see their children's (books') faces all over it!

So it's no wonder authors are affected by book reviews. Receiving a bad review is similar to a parent hearing that his or her child is stupid or ugly. Receiving a good review is comparable to his or her child being named class valedictorian.

Authors feel shame, anger, frustration, and pride over their books, just like parents with their children.

In fact, here are ten ways being an author is like being a parent.

1. For an author, releasing a new book is equivalent to announcing a new baby's arrival.

2. Authors love to show off their new "babies" (i.e. book covers) as much as parents love to show off their children's pictures.

3. Even though authors want to flaunt their "babies" (i.e. books), they also want to protect them from all negativity in the world (i.e. bad reviews).

4. Authors carry each one of their children (i.e. stories) around for months before seeing them be born.

5. Authors are proud of their "babies" when they succeed, and embarrassed—but still love them—when they fail.

6. Authors, often unknowingly, transfer their own personality traits on to their "babies" (i.e. the characters in their books).

7. Authors get the privilege of naming their "babies" anything they choose—and often take a lot of heat for choosing the wrong names.

8. Authors, like parents, always think their "babies" are the best in the world and that everyone should love them as much.

9. Authors' legacies live on through their "babies."

10. An author's mood at any given time can range between sad, happy, nervous, embarrassed, and proud, depending on recent interactions with their "babies" – Yep, sounds like parenthood to me!

Authorhood – The (other) best worst job in the world!

TIP 325: *Grow a spine, grow your fan base*

As authors, we must develop two hard shells that cover certain parts of our bodies—one that shields our spine, and the other, our hearts. We write what comes from our minds and our hearts and then throw those words out into the world to be scrutinized, commented on, and often chewed up and spit out by strangers.

This can be a bit disheartening and hard to take. In fact, many a promising author has given up on writing because of bad reviews for their books. They assume they don't have what it takes to be a writer.

I personally enjoy reading bios of famous authors—to discover their backstories. I like to learn how they broke into fame, where they came from, and how many times they were rejected before they found their golden ticket. It keeps me motivated in my writing. Did you know J.K. Rowling was on welfare while writing the first Harry Potter book?

I must admit, I was the type of author who listened with her heart when I first began publishing. I took it personally every time I received a not-so-perfect comment on my books from readers or editors.

Thankfully, being the researcher I am, I decided to learn as much as possible about all the aspects of writing, publishing, and marketing. Of course, I'm still learning, but I have come a long way.

Authors who wish to make it in this business must develop thick skin. You must be open to suggestions for improving your work—

especially when they come from your readers. Now, I'm not saying you should change your book every time a reader offers a suggestion; but, if you are seeing similar comments come across in reviews, take them into consideration for improving your book. Or you may choose to implement those things into your future books.

For instance, some of my readers who have reviewed my second novel *Unsevered* have mentioned that they felt the love story toward the end was rushed because I didn't go into detail about her (spoiler alert) second love interest. I can understand their viewpoint, but this is a particular part of my book that I will not be changing. Simply because, I wrote it this way for a purpose. My female character had already found the love of her life once; and even though she found someone else to love in the end, no one could replace her first love. I didn't want to taint the uniqueness and specialness of their bond.

So, in conclusion, listen to your readers and editors—if they have a valid point. Don't take everything personally. Open yourself up to critiques. Notice I didn't say criticism. I feel there is a fine line between the two. Critiquing involves helping someone improve. Criticism only tears them down without suggesting anything to help.

Write from the heart, but edit and make changes from your spine. Hmm, do you think it's a coincidence that the spine is the strongest part of a book? Perhaps it makes sense for it to also be the strongest part of the author.

TIP 326: Are you a starving artist?

I'm sure many of you have heard that phrase before—starving artist. Well, it's only an idiom. It's not meant to be taken in the literal sense. What we put into our bodies affects our brains, so especially as writers, it's important to keep ourselves nourished.

Here are 9 ways to stay healthy and keep your brain sharp:

1. Yoga: I adore yoga. There are so many benefits gained from this ancient form of exercise and meditation, I don't have room to list them all. A few ways it helps the body are: calming and centering the mind, strengthening the heart and organs, opening the airways to ensure adequate and proper breathing, and strengthening the muscles.

2. Eat breakfast: It's been proven that breakfast is the most important meal of the day. Many people choose to not eat breakfast, and most of those people struggle with their weight. The reason breakfast plays such a big role in nutrition is because it's the first thing the body receives after a long rest. During nighttime sleep is when the body is repairing itself from the day, therefore it uses a lot of energy. To have that energy restored (i.e. prevent brain fog, fatigue, and dizziness) the body must receive nourishment after sleep. Even if you "aren't a breakfast person" it's best to at least put some form of protein in your body within the first hour of waking—a tablespoon of peanut butter, one hard-boiled egg, or even a whole-grain waffle. Many people who aren't "breakfast people" substitute with coffee. While one cup of coffee per day is good for the body, most coffee drinkers gulp down several cups of sugar-laden coffee per day and have less-than-desirable eating habits.

3.   Drink plenty of water: Water is the number one thing a body needs. This magic liquid is involved with nearly every process in the body. If you aren't able to drink 6-8 (recommended) glasses per day, drop a bit of water flavor or fresh fruit in there. And though it may be a bit more expensive, drink bottled water. Some people, like me, have to have measurable goals. I know if I gulp down at least four 16.9oz water bottles per day, I'm staying hydrated—or at least meeting the minimum requirement.

4.   Get adequate sleep: This is a tough one for writers because our brains are always going, it seems. We have voices in our heads and lines of prose that torture us until we get up and write them down. But, as I mentioned before, during nighttime sleep is when the healing/repairing process takes place. So, at least 6-8 hours per night is recommended. And, keeping a regular schedule is best to keep your body's circadian rhythm on track.

5.   Enjoy sodas and sweets only on occasion. These sodium and sugar-laden foods are enemies of healthy brain activity. Too much sodium can affect the absorption of the water that your body needs. Too much sugar can slow your brain's ability to maintain memory and slow your insulin, which is what helps your body process thoughts and emotions—two very important aspects of writing!

6.   Exercise your brain: The internet is inundated with digital games which strengthen connections in the brain. However, if you've been sitting at a computer for several hours in a row without a break, the last thing you need is more screen time. Instead, try to do a physical puzzle, color, draw, or write on paper for a while. Go for a walk; connecting with nature calms the mind as well. Look through a family photo album. Organize something in your home. Play with a Rubix Cube, play a board game with someone, or read a paperback book. Every now and then it's okay to take a break and watch TV, but remember that it involves more screen time. Plus, it does

nothing good for the brain. Listen to music, and dance around the house while you clean.

7. Stay connected with friends and family—the ones you like, anyway. (smile)

8. Don't hang around negative people who are always complaining about their stations in life or are always looking for someone to blame. And, spread your socializing time out between social media and connections with tangible people. Meet up with a friend once a week. Join a physical book club. Go to church. Call a friend on the phone—not text! Go outside and play with your kids.

9. Get a massage: As writers, we spend a great many hours at a desk with our necks craned to look at a screen. Tension builds up in our shoulders and back. Not only can massage address these problems, it has so many more benefits. Did you know that the feet contain reflex points that affect every gland and organ in the body? So, not only can massage relieve physical pain and stress, it can improve brain function that affects all other parts of the body.

10. Get regular check-ups. This is especially important as you age, to keep your heart, eyes, lungs, and other organs healthy. Stay current with your eye doctor and general practitioner, as well as getting mammograms or other cancer-preventing tests done as needed. If parts of your body don't work, it gives you one more obstacle to battle when you want to write.

I've just listed nine ways to keep your brain healthy as a writer. Remember, what you do for your body today pays off in the years to come. One of my greatest fears is having mental issues when I'm older. I want to do everything I can to preserve my brain function.

TIP 327: Sometimes you just have to say "no"!

This tip covers a topic that I'll bet many of you struggle with in your writing career, or even in your everyday life … whether you want to admit it or not.

Some people have an extremely difficult time saying "no," out of fear that they will be missing out on something or disappointing someone. I can honestly say that I've agreed to projects that my heart wasn't into, and I've had others agree to help me with projects, and I could tell their hearts weren't into it either.

Opportunities are simply options, not obligations. They are there to teach us discernment and build our confidence. Just because we are offered the chance to do something, doesn't mean we have to, or even should every time.

The main problem with never turning down an offer is that most people agree to these "opportunities" out of obligation, rather than passion. Therefore, the project only receives a halfway effort, or at least not the best effort possible. If your heart isn't into a project, it shows. If you have limited knowledge about a project topic, that is eventually revealed as well.

Many authors will accept anything that comes their way, whether it fits into their writing career path, schedule, or even genre. Their train of thought is usually focused on "exposure" more than anything else. Unfortunately, many of these endeavors are nothing more than a waste of the author's time—time that could be spent writing, researching, or marketing elsewhere.

Being a mother of three, a full-time child-care provider, managing my blog and now a new website to promote other authors, I've learned that I can't do it all. Moreover, I'm not meant to do it all. I had to teach myself that even though I may be missing something by not participating in every opportunity that comes my way, I'm not missing anything that was meant for me. I've gotten good at trusting my gut, and if I don't get completely excited about a project, or I lose passion during the project, I trust myself to know it's time to move on.

Most authors are juggling other jobs and familial responsibilities as well. Our time is precious, so we should protect it and learn to use it wisely.

Don't think that you have to agree to every Facebook takeover or anthology project that's offered to you. Don't sign up for every single writing contest you discover, unless you know you have the time and passion to see it through and meet the deadline.

Only choose projects that excite you, projects that you know you can commit to fully, projects that will be worth your time, efforts, and money (if money is involved). Otherwise, you may find that you've spread yourself too thin and it will show in your work.

Wouldn't you rather have a few projects that show your best work than a dozen or so that only reveal your minimal talents?

TIP 328: Keeping up with the Joneses (comparing your success to others')

One quick way to lose your motivation and zest as an author is to compare yourself to people who are more successful than you, especially celebrities.

Authors don't reach their goals all at the same time. Some take years to write one book while others produce four books per year.

It can be disheartening to witness someone else reaching his/her goals before you, but there are a few things to keep in mind when this happens.

1. Not everyone has the same family structure or support system. You may be caring for little ones while the authors you admire most for their success are in their retirement phase of life. Or they may not even have children. Or, if they do have children, perhaps they have full-time nannies or housekeepers to take up some of the domestic responsibilities. I've even met authors whose spouses work full time and manage the house so they can focus on writing. Everyone's familial situation is different.

2. Not everyone has the same budget. You may not have the money to hire a full-time nanny or housekeeper, or book publicist, whereas many authors you know may have a full team of people behind them, handling all their marketing and event scheduling. They may have the means to spend thousands of dollars on publicity and media events, while you are struggling to put food on the table.

3. You may not be as ready for the level of success you crave as you think you are. You may have some personal issues that

need to be addressed before you can devote the time and energy it takes to manage that level of success or stardom.

4. Just because you have goals you'd like to achieve, doesn't mean that those particular goals are part of your future plans. They might not be the right goals for your life path, and you don't know it yet. Some things are out of our control.

5. Some of the authors who seem to "have it all" in life may be putting on a facade, especially if you're hearing about it on Facebook. (Don't trust everything you read on social media.) They may be making money hand over fist but might be miserable in their personal lives, or have no one to share their fortune with because they've alienated everyone from their lives.

6. Some authors save money for years, and live on an extremely tight budget to be able to pour every extra dollar into their publishing endeavors. We each have choices to make with our money.

Basically, before you judge (whether giving too much credit, or not enough credit to) other authors who seem to be where you want to be, remember that you don't know their life stories or all that transpires in their daily lives. You are not them. You have your own situation, your own family, and your own dreams to chase.

As long as you are taking steps (tiny as they may be) in the right direction toward your goals and dreams, and producing your best effort with each endeavor along the way, that's all you can expect from yourself.

It will all come together in good time. You will be in a different phase of your life one day as well.

TIP 329: Are you ready to write that?

This tip might be somewhat of a tough pill to swallow for some because the truth doesn't always go down easily. However, that doesn't make it any less necessary to hear.

As an author, you must be completely honest with yourself about your writing skills, knowledge, and strengths. If you are struggling to write a particular piece, it could mean that you simply aren't ready to write it.

This doesn't mean that you won't be ready at some point in the future. Many aspects of great writing involve the right timing.

Perhaps you haven't learned enough about the topic you are writing about.

Perhaps you can't pull the right words out of your soul to tell that story because it's too raw and emotional for you. (too close to home at this time)

Perhaps you aren't the right person to write that particular piece, because it's not authentic coming from you. It's not something you are knowledgeable about or passionate enough about.

Perhaps some other events are meant to take place in your life that will influence you in writing a better version of this story.

What can you do if a story isn't coming easily to you?

1. Write something else. Get your mind on something else. The answer to that plot twist may come to you when you least expect it.

2. Research more about your topic. Learn everything you can so you are able to write about it in an authentic voice.

3. Step away from it. Even if you go do something completely non-writing related, that may provide the perfect life experience you need to be able to write that piece with authenticity.

4. Perhaps you are trying to write someone else's story, and you are simply meant to be a guide for that person. Search your soul to discover whose story it really is.

5. Read similar stories from that genre for inspiration. Writers improve their skills through reading.

6. Give it time. If you are trying to write a memoir, autobiography, or even a fictional piece based on a personal experience, perhaps it's too soon and you haven't worked through your emotions on it well enough to articulate your thoughts.

7. Seek critique partners. Offer what you have so far to see what they think. Seek out honest, trustworthy people who will tell you what you need to hear, not what you want to hear.

Above all, don't stop writing, and don't think you're a bad writer because you can't quite get that one piece.

I had to take three months off from writing my second novel *Unsevered* before I was able to finish it. Many times, I thought I was not going to be able to finish it because I couldn't quite get a timeline portion figured out. That break was exactly what I needed. Now that novel has won several awards and is nominated for another, I'm so thankful I waited.

TIP 330: Sharing your WIP (work in progress)

We all get excited about sharing our works in progress, especially if we've published other books and our "fans" are waiting for our next one to come out.

The problem is: some authors share too much too soon. For instance, some send their first few chapters to several beta readers to get their feedback, which can be a good thing or bad thing, depending on who the beta readers are.

One advantage to having several beta readers is that multiple people offer multiple viewpoints. The con is that multiple people offer multiple viewpoints. What I mean by this is: too many hands in the cookie jar can leave a crumbled mess.

Many authors try to accommodate all of their beta readers' suggestions and end up losing their unique voice in the writing by fluffing up the book with too much unnecessary content.

In one of the tips in my upcoming book Before You Publish (Volume I): Tips on grammar, writing, and editing, I talked about beta readers and alpha readers. Though it's important to have these people on our team, it's just as crucial that we choose the right ones, and take their suggestions into consideration, while realizing that they are not the final say in our stories. We are. And we should trust our instincts if something doesn't feel quite right.

Another thing authors do in sharing too much too soon, like excerpts of upcoming books at the end of previously published ones, is offer part of a story that never comes to fruition, or one that changes dramatically. I did this and I wish I hadn't. My story changed quite a bit once published. I don't think my readers noticed (or cared) much once my second one came out, but I knew the wrong content was there and it still bugs me to this day to know I have those books out there, and even a few printed copies in stock. I don't even want to sell them to anyone.

So in conclusion, be careful when sharing too much about your current WIP. It may end up changing drastically, or it may not ever be published. Once the book has been written and edited at least once, then it's probably a safe time to share.

TIP 331: Are you a one-book wonder?

If writing is to become your sole source of income, the best way to capitalize on that skill is to produce multiple books. The more books you offer, the more avenues of income you can attain. As well, if you write in various genres, you can create multiple paths to success and wealth.

Here are five reasons why offering more than one title can increase your income:

1. Many readers are loyal to their favorite authors. When they read something they like, they typically want to read everything by that author, if it's a genre they are interested in. I've had readers email me and ask what other titles I've written that they might enjoy.

2. If various genre writings are offered, the author can reach a variety of reader types. Nonfiction, mystery, thriller, romance, etc.

3. Writing in a variety of genres allows the author to prove his/her writing talents to readers. In other words, it proves that he/she is a great writer … no matter the topic.

4. If an author produces outstanding books in various genres, he/she may be presented with multiple opportunities for speaking engagements, media appearances, or article submissions. As well, the author may be offered a job teaching certain aspects of the writing craft.

5. The more books an author pens, typically his/her writing skills improve. Therefore, publishing multiple titles allows the

author to hone his/her craft, and writing in various genres allows an author to adapt to different writing styles. Nonfiction and fiction writing differs greatly in tone, verbiage, and presentation.

Some authors transition between fiction and non-fiction genres with ease, often to the point that readers forget what genre they are reading.

Most authors write, or began writing, for the joy of the craft. The ones who truly enjoy playing with words have no trouble producing several titles, and that enthusiasm shows in their writing.

Authors should try to offer various types of writing pieces to build multiple fan bases. The more options you provide to readers of all genres, the more money-making opportunities you create.

TIP 332: Writing dreams Vs. Writing goals

I think we all have dreams. Dreams are easy. There are no commitments or boundaries to adhere to.

But goals? Not everyone has them.

And there is a difference between dreams and goals.

Dreams are essentially ideas about things we'd like to have or accomplish in the future. There are no limits, boundaries, or time constraints involved in our dreams. They are broad visions, such as wishing to be a millionaire or a best-selling author one day. Sure, these things aren't impossible; many people have done them. But they aren't practical. Dreams like these don't come true overnight. They typically take many years of hard work, and often, simply knowing the right people.

Goals, on the other hand, do have guidelines. There are boundaries and time constraints involved, which are necessary to keep us on track and allow us to reach our goals.

There are two types of goals: short term and long term. Both types play key roles in helping us move forward in life.

Short-term goals involve tasks we strive to achieve on a daily, weekly, monthly, or yearly basis. They are measurable and attainable—realistic. Deadlines give us a sense of urgency. Many writers, myself included, find comfort and security in setting and attaining short-term goals. Doing so allows them to feel productive, as if they are getting one step closer to their ultimate dream.

Here are some short-term goals a writer might set, broken down into daily, weekly, and monthly, and yearly: (I personally consider yearly goals long-term based, but some consider them short-term goals.)

Daily:
- write 500 words per day
- check and respond to emails twice a day
- write one chapter per day
- contact one new blogger per day
- write on my blog once per day
- write for one hour without interruptions
- respond to social media interactions twice per day – schedule social media posts
- edit 3-5 chapters per day

Weekly:
- contact one new blogger per week
- send one query letter out per week
- write a weekly blog post
- meet a word count or chapter count per week (3-5 chapters per week is a decent goal)
- devote 10 hours per week to writing
- edit 10-15 chapters per week
- research places to advertise your book
- complete an outline for a book
- send out a weekly newsletter

Monthly:
- send 3-5 query letters per month
- edit a book
- feature one author on your blog per month
- do one blog tour (for your books) per month
- research and contact one or two freelance writing companies about side work

- reach a milestone of likes/follows on social media – do a giveaway when you reach that number
- read at least one book (2-3 is even better) – reading is "studying" for your big test – writing your book
- learn one new way to market your books (reach your readers)
- send out a monthly newsletter

Yearly:
- publish 2-3 books per year (or whatever your "x" number is)
- enter 2 writing contests/awards programs for your books
- reach the #1 spot in your book's category (this could also be a monthly goal)
- attend one writer's conference per year
- write at least one thing out of your comfort zone
- have at least 2 book signings

Now let's look at some possible long-term goals for authors:

3-5 years from now:
- have at least 4 titles published (publishing 1-2 titles per year)
- be generating enough income from sales to replace half of your regular (traditional) income
- win a writing contest, or an award for your books
- be featured on the radio
- be featured on television
- have your books in a book store
- have a book signing in another state or country
- secure an agent or publisher
- create your own publishing team (your go-to people) – editor, designer/illustrator, formatting specialist, and publicist

6-10+ years:
- quit your J-O-B and become a full-time writer

- publish 3-5 titles per year
- travel the world teaching writing or marketing workshops
- be featured on television
- be featured on the radio
- reach the New York Times Bestseller's list

Notice some of the goals are listed more than once. That means, tomorrow is another day. If you don't reach your short-term goals in the desired time frame, they become long-term goals. If you keep plugging away, day by day at the little tasks, you will eventually reach your long-term goals as well (also known as lifetime goals).

It's important to note that your "tasks" must be writing-related and they must be productive activities which move you closer to your goals. In other words, your book will not make it to the #1 spot in its category if you don't market it and network online to reach your readers. As well, you won't ever make it on the radio or television if you don't take the time to research and contact the stations. It's called groundwork.

All these things you do each day are laying the foundation for your future in writing. Each word, line, paragraph, chapter, and story you write helps you improve your craft. Each blogger, reader, book-store owner, radio station, etc., you contact helps spread the word about your work.

Only you can do what it takes to live out your dreams. No one can do it for you. Write. Edit. Publish. Market. Connect.

TIP 333: 25 qualities most serious writers have in common

Just as there are certain things that athletes, musicians, and other professionals have in common, serious writers share common traits as well.

Here are at least twenty-five qualities most serious writers have in common:

1. We long to write full time, if we don't already. And if we do write full time, sometimes we resent it.

2. We constantly struggle with balancing our personal lives and our passion for writing.

3. We read a lot, and there never seems to be enough time in the day for the books we want to read.

4. We daydream. During our daily grind, our minds drift off to create characters, plots, or story ideas.

5. We had unrealistic expectations about the industry, and how much was truly involved in publishing a book.

6. We've developed enemies during our writing careers.

7. We've developed friendships during our writing careers.

8. We thought our friends and family members would love—and review—our books.

9. We've considered quitting.

10. We've gone back to writing, even if we did quit.

11. We've written crappy stories.

12. We've written great stories, and have been surprised by our talent.

13. We care about reviews, whether we admit it or not.

14. We secretly wish we could become rich and famous with our writing, but we also secretly worry that we wouldn't know how to handle that lifestyle. So really, we want fame and fortune with anonymity.

15. We feel guilty when we spend hours on end writing or editing, when we see our loved ones waiting in the wings.

16. We have read bad writing.

17. We have read amazing writing, and hated to admit it was better than ours.

18. We've all researched and learned something new about the industry, and ourselves, in our writing careers.

19. We enjoy social media interaction, but truly resent it for taking so much time and effort, when we'd rather be writing, or doing other things.

20. We talk about writing or books, in almost every conversation we have, even when we try not to.

21. We read blog posts and articles on writing, editing, publishing, and marketing.

22. We invest more money than we make on our books. (at least in the beginning)

23. We get discouraged and wonder if we're good enough to be published.

24. We are creative and find ways to get through "writer's block." In fact, we realize that "writer's block" is truly nothing more than lack of perseverance.

25. We all are people watchers, observers. And we use our life experiences to write authentically.

This list is not to make anyone feel selfish or guilty for having any of these qualities. Writers are a unique group of beings, because, not only do we feel things more deeply than most, but we have the talent to put those feelings into words that have power.

Owning these qualities, and recognizing that you are not alone in these feelings, will help you understand that it takes a special personality type to make it in this industry. Only the strong and determined survive, the ones who want it badly enough.

The fact that you struggle with balancing the various areas of your life, proves that you are loved and that you love deeply.

The fact that you write crappy stories, means you are brave enough to put your thoughts on paper, and eventually share them with the world.

The fact that you have quit writing because you thought you weren't good enough, shows that you know your limits, or priorities, as the case may be. But if you returned to writing, it shows that you have perseverance and passion.

So don't deny or rebuke these personality traits. They are the substance of YOU. Own them. Use them to help you grow as a person, and as a writer.

TIP 334: 10 ways writing a list can keep you from feeling "listless"

Time moves quickly these days, and many people lead "busy" lives. I prefer to call mine productive, instead. Busy people tend to do things that simply occupy their lives, whereas productive people often accomplish things that improve their lives.

Some people don't know how to take initiative, or don't have the personality to do so. That's why motivational speakers, how-to authors, and life coaches become so successful. People want to be productive and reach their goals, but they don't always know how to get started.

Want some free advice? Start with a list.

Here are ten ways writing a list can keep you from feeling "listless."

1. Lists provide a tangible visual aid. It's easy to forget or procrastinate on tasks that are mentally formed. But skipping out on, or putting off, something that is written on a physical to-do-list involves more conscious effort, and often—guilt!

2. Lists help organize and prioritize thoughts and desires. As the list materializes, the items are often categorized and rearranged by order of importance, many times subconsciously.

3. Lists are visual aids that can be shared to allow others to hold us accountable.

4. Lists provide instant gratification when items are completed and marked off.

5. Lists help people find things quickly. Shopping lists can easily be broken down into categories to make items easier to locate in a large space.

6. Lists can be delegated to other people when one is not able to accomplish everything alone.

7. Lists can be added to or taken away from, as needs and priorities change.

8. Lists allow large goals to be broken down into smaller, more-manageable tasks.

9. Lists that show several tasks completed (marked off) can provide a huge motivation for future goals to be attempted and reached.

10. Lists are completely customizable, since they derive from personal goals and preferences.

I use lists for practically everything I must get done—from grocery shopping, to cleaning my house, and even when doing taxes.

The next time you have a huge chore to accomplish, or simply one that seems major to YOU, try breaking it down into smaller, listed items. You might be amazed at how accomplished you feel—which, in turn, motivates you to do more.

TIP 335: Do you have a book in you?

This tip is for all the aspiring authors out there—those who haven't written their first book.

How long have you dreamed of becoming an author? Since you were old enough to write? Or did you just recently discover your love of the written word? Perhaps you've never put much thought into it but have been told by others that you should write a book. Whatever the case, however you reached the point of considering writing that first piece, you need to simply get the words out of your head and down on paper.

I firmly believe that anyone can write, but not everyone can write well. That's okay. That's what editors are for. Only YOU have lived your life and had those experiences, so only YOU can tell your stories.

Here are some ideas for books YOU could write:

- Are you a teacher? Write books that are targeted to the age group you teach (picture books, middle-grade fiction, YA novels). Who better than YOU—the one who knows these kids better than most of their parents.

- Are you a stay-home mom or dad? Write a book about how to organize a home, manage an activities schedule with kids, or how to teach kids their basic concepts (colors, shapes, letters, etc.). You don't need a college degree to do this. Offer a recipe book filled with kid-friendly snacks and meals. Write a book about how to stay on a budget while feeding a family with only one income.

- Are you a doctor? Write a book about the journey of a medical student from classroom to operating table. Or write a book about your top twenty surgeries. Are you a lawyer? Write a legal thriller.

- Are you a waitress? Write a thriller about a waitress who is stalked by a regular customer. Or write a story about a waitress who worked her way up to owning her own restaurant.

- Are you in the military? Who better than to write a military thriller, or an autobiography about life behind enemy lines?

- Are you a musician? Write an autobiography about life on the road as a performer, or write a general-fiction story about a musician who gets a big break on Broadway or performing at Carnegie hall.

- Are you a world traveler? You have tons of amazing stories to tell. A non-fiction book The World Through My Eyes or something like that would be great. Pictures would be helpful in a book of this nature.

- Are you a scientist? Write a sci-fi story or a medical thriller.

- Are you a farmer? Who would be able to write a better book than you on how to grow tasty produce, when to plant the seeds, or how much to water a garden?

- Are you a pilot or flight attendant? My, the people you've met along the way, and the places you've visited. You've probably even had a few scares in your career.

- Have you ever: had a baby, been married or divorced, learned a new skill, had a frightening experience, accomplished a goal or overcome a fear, traveled to a new place, gotten an exciting job, gone to the circus, gone to a fair, worked in a hospital?

If you've lived, you've had experiences that you can write about. So whether you've been agonizing about writing a book, you've been told by others that you should write one, or it's something that never crossed your mind until now, give it a try. Get the words down on paper. You never know who needs your book, whose life can be changed by your words.

I personally have always been a writer, from the young age of ten. I had my first poem published in a local newspaper and became addicted to the power of my words. Though I've always written songs, poems, and short pieces, I didn't publish my first book until four years ago. But I haven't looked back since.

TIP 336: All by myself

(13 ways to combat isolation as a writer)

Many authors are introverts, so being alone actually rejuvenates them. However, some are extroverts who are fueled by social interaction. Extremes of either of these personalities can cause problems with writing.

It's a common misconception that all introverts like being alone constantly; most simply need "some" alone time. It doesn't mean they don't want to be around people altogether. All humans need attention, affection, nurturing, and interaction, but some prefer to have it in smaller doses than others.

Writing can be quite a lonely occupation/hobby for some people, especially extroverts, which may explain the constant distraction of social media. It's not all about marketing. Authors are human and need to feel connected to the rest of the world. The problem is, social media can suck the life out of us sometimes—especially if we come across something sad or disturbing. As well, it can go the opposite direction and draw us in for hours, interrupting our creative flow, resulting in "writer's block" as some call it.

Here are 13 ways to combat that "all by myself" feeling that can often make us almost want to "talk back" to our characters:

1. After a long day of writing, call a friend or allow yourself an hour to "catch up" on social media.

2. Go for a walk, outside, not on a treadmill. Hopefully you'll run into one or two humans.

3. Connect with your spouse or kids as often as you can. This goes back to setting specific writing times and letting them know when you are available.

4. Take up a hobby other than writing, one that requires you to be around other people—in small doses if need be. (the gym, yoga, church, sports, etc.)

5. Visit a friend or relative.

6. If you can't call someone (loud kids in the background, etc.) text them or message them on social media. Sometimes scrolling through your timeline (covertly) can make you feel as if you are keeping up with the world around you. It doesn't always have to involve interaction.

7. Take your kids to the park. Bonus: you can get some "people watching" in as well, for your stories.

8. Create a podcast on YouTube to interact with people.

9. Go read to kids at a local school or daycare center, especially if you write children's books.

10. Connect with authors (book clubs, social media groups) who are going through the same emotions and writing challenges.

11. Join a physical book club. Reading is required there, and that's essentially studying for your own books.

12. Go have a couple of drinks with a friend, or alone. (Either way, you are still around people.) Bonus: the bartender most likely has some interesting story material to share with you—inadvertently, of course.

13. Volunteer at a local shelter, orphanage, or retirement home on occasion.

Many people who read our books are truly lonely and depressed. Our words can be lifelines for them. But sometimes we need to take care of ourselves and make sure we stay plugged in to the world. How can we help our readers who feel this way if we feel the same? We need to be rays of hope for them.

TIP 337: Living with non-writers
(How to love those who don't love what you do)

Have any of you who are authors noticed that your circle of friends grew smaller once you published your book(s)? I'm not only talking about the friends who still haven't reviewed, much less read, your books. I'm referring to the ones who seemed to have disappeared once you began even talking about your books.

Don't feel alone. It happens to many authors.

In fact, it happens to many people in general, for several reasons:

- Some people feel threatened when their friends aren't on the same "level" (socially, financially, or career-wise) as they are.

- Some people back off because they are afraid you will ask them to read/review your book and they are afraid of being honest with you if they end up not liking it. In other words, they don't want to be put in an awkward position.

- Some people feel threatened by anyone who has goals.

- Some people are selfish and only want their friends to be happy if they are happy. (It's the same with the friends who only want you to be single when they are single.)

- Some people aren't interested in anything to do with reading or writing. Yes. They do exist. (Breathe. Breathe.)

Many authors enjoy talking about all things related to books and writing. However, their friends and family do not.

Sure, they may be supportive and buy—and if the planets align, maybe even review—our books. But this doesn't mean that they will ever be as invested in the process as we authors are. It's not their passion. They don't lose sleep over a certain line of a story. They aren't tormented by the fate of characters. Even if they are avid readers, it doesn't mean they care about the writing process as much as authors do.

So how do we deal with the ones we love, who don't love what we do?

- Don't bring up the subject of your writing or anything related to writing unless asked. And even then, learn to gauge if the person asking is truly interested in learning about it, or if he/she is simply being polite.

- If you do mention your writing, be sure to talk about other topics as well.

- Ask your friends/loved ones about their lives. Remember, whatever is going on in their lives is just as important to them as your writing is to you.

- Don't ask your friends/loved ones to read or review your books. If they offer, great. Otherwise, leave that to avid readers who will appreciate your work.

- Don't try to coerce your friends/loved ones into reading your book by giving them free copies, thinking you are doing them a favor. If they are truly interested, they will ask you how to buy a copy to support you.

- Don't hold it against them if they don't want to read or even talk about your books. Keep in mind that they knew you before you began publishing, and that person is who they built a relationship with, not the author you became. Don't take it personally if they don't want to talk about things in your life that don't involve them.

- Remember to balance your time between your writing and your friends/loved ones. It's hard. As authors, we get an idea in our heads and want to run with it, damned the rest of the world when we're in the writing zone. But as humans, we can't do that too often or we will burn some bridges we don't want to burn. Make time for your spouse, other than getting him/her to read your latest synopsis. Make time for your children. Yes, it's great for them to see you going for your dreams and goals, but don't make them feel as if they aren't as special or important to you as your writing. No matter what book I publish, writing award I win, or celebrity status I ever reach, my ultimate achievement in life is being a great mom to my children, and wife to my husband. They will always come first.

- Don't correct your friends/loved ones' grammar on social media or in person, unless you have that kind of relationship with him or her. No one likes a know-it-all. Whether they are being lazy or simply naive, it's not your place to judge them or correct them.

- Don't forget to thank your closest family and friends who do support your writing journey, whether it's your spouse who cares for the kids so you can write, your best friend who reads your worst crap before you rewrite it, or your children who learn to wait "just a few more minutes" to eat dinner because you are trying to wrap up a chapter. Just because they don't materially participate in your writing, doesn't mean they don't play a huge role in your process. Thank them in your books, and in person.

- Don't buy books for your friends/loved ones who you know don't enjoy reading, thinking you will convince them how great it is. Or worse, buy them books you know they won't enjoy so they will give the books to you. That's just wrong. (smile)

It's hard for us authors to remember sometimes that there are people in this vast world who don't enjoy and appreciate the written word as much as we do. When I hear someone say, "I simply don't enjoy reading," I want to claw my eyes out. But it's not my place to force it on them or judge them for their lack of interest.

So, keep your relationships with those you love by remembering what brought you together in life in the first place. Focus on that and let them know you cherish their presence in your life … even if they don't enjoy all the same things you do.

TIP 338: We're human before we're anything else

This tip is quite personal for me, and not easy to write, as it derived from a blog post I submitted in the segment last year. However, I'm a person of integrity and honesty, so I feel a strong need to offer these words. I'm sure some of you will run into a similar situation in your writing or blogging career, and it's important to have the tools to handle it.

We are all human. We all make mistakes. We've all been misinformed on topics, and have misunderstood concepts.

I released a blog post that was a perfect example of this.

I thought I had my facts straight, and I felt strongly about the examples and tips I offered in that post. But I was wrong. I apparently hadn't considered the situation from all angles before sharing my thoughts. And since it was a teaching segment, I could not, in good conscience, keep that post as part of this segment.

Instead, I admitted my fault, and I offered a replacement post.

This may happen at some point in your career as well. What should you do?

My advice? Don't fake it 'til you make it. Own it. Let your blog followers know that you're human and you simply misspoke. Don't try to cover it up—or worse yet—argue about it, unless you know you are right.

This is how you earn trust with your followers.

I'm not offering this tip to say that you should retract every statement you make, simply to avoid conflict or objection. You should stand strong in your convictions, if your information is correct. But if your information has been proven incorrect, it's best to admit your mistake to your followers and move on with a new topic.

Humility is yet another quality you should keep handy in this business.

TIP 339: Answering questions about being an author

Many authors feel uncomfortable talking about what they do. Sure, they enjoy talking about books by others they've read, but they have a hard time starting conversations or answering questions about their own published titles. Perhaps they feel as if they are bragging, or they worry they will be judged.

Whatever the reason you aren't talking up your books to others, you must learn to get past this if you want to be successful, because word of mouth is your most powerful ally as a published author.

Keep in mind, just because you talk up your books, it doesn't mean you're obligated to divulge every bit of information about the business or your writing process.

I've seen multiple posts on "questions to never ask an author," but the fact that these posts exist doesn't mean that readers, friends, and family won't continue to ask these questions.

With that said, here are 10 typical questions you may hear as an author, and acceptable answers to keep your party interested while not divulging all your secrets.

1. How is the novel coming?

    A. Acceptable answers:

    B. It's really coming together nicely. I'm excited about the plot twist I'm writing.

    C. I decided to take a break and work on a few short stories instead. I'm always flooded with ideas. (whether it's true or not)

2. Don't you ever run out of things to write about?

   A. Not really. I always have a few projects going at once.

   B. I can write about pretty much anything

3. How many books have you sold? (An author's least favorite question) It's amazing the level of audacity people exhibit in asking this question, one they would not even think of asking any other professional. But you can still answer gracefully.

   A. It varies from month to month, but I've been quite surprised by the response to my books.

   B. It's hard to keep up, I have my books listed and featured in so many places. They do quite well. (be vague)

4. What are you working on right now?

   A. The answers to this can vary. You can always say you're working on several pieces, or you can use this chance to talk up your book.

   B. If it's a second (or subsequent) novel you've been working on and your first one did quite well, you can say, "I'm focusing on marketing my first one for a while, but I am writing my second one every chance I get."

5. Have you written anything I've heard of?

   A. (You don't have to scream the words "self-published" here.) Instead say, "Perhaps. Do you read romance (your writing genre)?" If they say yes, then you can say, "Hmm, I'm surprised because it's been out for a while and it's doing quite well on Amazon. It's listed pretty much everywhere online."

6. Where do you get ideas for your writing?

   A. Sometimes my stories are inspired by real people I know, but other times I pull them directly from my brain.

   B. I read a lot and sometimes put my own unique twist on stories I like.

7. I started writing a book as well. Would you mind taking a look at it? (If you're afraid of it jeopardizing your friendship/relationship)

   A. I would but I'm super busy with my books at the moment. I do have some beta-reader friends who might have time to check it out.

   B. I'm a bit tied up with my current WIP at the moment, but I may have time later. (if you want to avoid it or put it off)

8. What's your real job?

   A. Writing is a real job. I write real words in real books. (and then laugh)

   B. I'm blessed enough to be able to make a good living at doing something I love. By the way, how much money do you make? – just kidding. Don't say that.

9. How do I go about getting published?

   A. I would suggest you do a lot of research online before deciding if you want to self-publish or be traditionally published. (be vague)

B. I didn't take the traditional route so my situation is unique. There are a lot of resources online about the industry. Good luck! (be courteous and helpful but still a bit vague)

10. Can I get a free copy of your book? (or "I'll read it if I can get it for free." Otherwise known as the friends/family discount)

A. I don't give my work away for free, but it's reasonably priced on Amazon and other book retail sites.

B. Sure, can I get a free lipstick from you (Mary Kay consultant), free haircut and color (hairdresser), manicure (nail technician)? See where I'm going with this? We don't ask others for free things so why are we okay as authors to give our books away? (But don't really answer this way, unless you're brave enough, or don't really like the person.)

These are only a few of the questions authors hear frequently. Writing is one of those unique professions that gives the impression of not having a "real" job. Those of us in the industry know the truth. Writing is a never-ending, mind-swallowing, gut-wrenching, nerve-wrecking, and at times—frustrating, time-consuming sinkhole that only the not-so-sane people of the world even attempt much less stick with. But it can also be rewarding and validating. Don't let the naysayers and busy bodies of the world pull you away from your craft or make you feel embarrassed about what you do.

Words have power. The power to entertain, inform, and heal. Never feel as if you're bragging too much about your gift or that you aren't a "professional author" because your name isn't on the New York Times Bestseller list. Claim your fame and hold your head high. You are a creator of something out of nothing. That's special. That's worth talking about!

TIP 340: Retreat and recharge to write better

Do you ever feel that if you could "just get away from it all for a while" your writing would flow like honey? Writing is not easy on the brain or the body. Sitting for long periods of time, working on a story, can wreak havoc on your muscles. And constantly brainstorming or researching for your story or other writing projects can be emotionally exhausting. Not to mention, familial obligations and distractions can thwart our efforts.

Perhaps all you need to gain a bit of perspective is a writer's retreat.

I know of one author who, just this summer, attended a writer's retreat in Vermont on a huge farm out in the middle of nowhere for seven days. The ironic thing is, the entire farm was set up for this retreat. The attendees spent most of the day in their rooms working on their writing. They had meals together, classes together, and sat together in the evenings to critique one another's work. All expenses were included in the trip price, which was, I believe around $1500. But the coolest thing about this place was that the people who set up the event were literary agents and publishers who offered a publishing contest. The winner of the contest received a publishing deal at the end of the event!

Here is the link for the site if you'd like to check this place out. http://whenwordscountretreat.com/

If you might be near the New Jersey area sometime soon, perhaps you'd like to try this writer's retreat? http://murphywriting.com/writing-getaways.html

This lady offers several writing retreats around New Mexico and the California area. Some events include yoga. I would so be there for that one if I could!
http://lauradavis.net/writing-retreats/

This lady travels to Vermont, Mexico, and California offering retreats for writers, and her site has impressive testimonials.
https://jenniferlouden.com/workshops-retreats/

Do you live near my peachy state (Georgia)? If so, you might like to try the writer's retreat in beautiful, historic Savannah!
http://www.ossabawwritersretreat.org/

And all I can say about this one is ... PARIS! Who wouldn't want to go to Paris ... to write?!
http://www.pariswritersretreat.com/

There you have six very different writers' retreats to choose from.

You are welcome to Google more. These are the ones I found most interesting. You can bank on between $1000 – $3000 per retreat, depending on where you go and how long you stay, but most of the trips are all-inclusive, which is nice. And if you can't afford to "get away" on a writer's retreat, perhaps you can create your own retreat right at home. Send the kids and spouse away for one weekend, light up those candles, and get busy writing!

TIP 341: Learn to take a compliment

How many of you have ever had a fan or another author give you a compliment like: "You are such a talented writer." Or: "You are so good at what you do."?

How do you respond?

Many of you, especially those who are shy or don't have a great deal of confidence, will respond with something like: "You really liked it?" Or: "Oh, I'm not that good. I just enjoy writing." Or: "I'm an amateur, but (author's name) is much better than me."

Why do you do this to yourselves?

Believe it or not, when people offer compliments, all they are truly seeking is acknowledgement of their words and opinions. That person was kind enough to take the time to extend a few words of encouragement or gratitude to you, and when you respond with comments such as those above, it can make him or her feel embarrassed or foolish for being so outspoken.

Many people find it quite difficult to compliment others, so when they do find the courage to, their words need to be acknowledged. When you don't validate someone's compliment, it's as if saying, "Oh, you don't have good taste." Or: "You don't really know what you're talking about."

How would it make you feel to hear those words?

Here are a few things to ask yourself as an author:
- Did you work hard on your book, give it your best effort?

- Did you spend a great deal of time and money publishing your book?
- Do you want readers/fans to enjoy your work and let you know they enjoyed it?
- Do you want to be recognized as a professional in the industry? Do you want to be considered a talented writer?
- Have you ever wanted to write your favorite author, even a fellow author, to express how much you loved his or her book?

If you answered yes to these questions, then you do want to be complimented on your work. You simply might not have learned how to accept words of praise.

Here are a few ways to respond to a fan:
- Thank you so much for taking the time to read my book and letting me know your thoughts. I truly appreciate it.
- Thank you for your kind words. I put a great deal of time and effort into that novel and I'm happy to hear it's paying off with my readers.
- I appreciate you taking the time to share those encouraging words with me.
- You're very kind. I appreciate your thoughtful words.
- Thank you. I'm glad you enjoyed my writing.
- It means a lot to me that you took the time to read my work and share your thoughts with me.

Basically, in any way you feel most comfortable, show your gratitude! You can be humble and secretly proud of your accomplishments at the same time, but there is a fine line between confidence and conceitedness. Truly mature individuals learn how to walk this line with grace and dignity.

How to respond to a fellow author's compliments:

- That means a lot coming from a fellow author. I admire your writing as well. (If you've checked it out, that I appreciate your kind words. What genre do you write? I may be interested in reading it.

- Thank you for that kind sentiment. It's always nice to connect with a fellow author.

- Thank you so much. I'm always happy to meet a fellow wordsmith.

- Thanks. It's nice to know that my work is appreciated.

Gauge the setting and the demeanor of the person complimenting you, especially if it's a face-to-face encounter. Online, you may need to incorporate a few emoticons to express proper tone. Don't be stuffy in your response to someone who is using all caps and a multitude of emoticons or punctuation.

Ex:
Fan:
OMG! I just finished your book. You are an amazing author!!! I will be sure to check out your other books in this series and tell all my friends about you!!! ε

Author:

Stuffy/boring response: I appreciate you taking the time to read my book. You are most welcome.

Acceptable response but not the most exciting: So glad you enjoyed my book. And I appreciate you sharing it with your friends!

Most exciting response (for this type of fan): Thanks so much for those inspiring words! It thrills me to know you enjoyed my work and will be sharing it with your friends. This totally makes my day! (add a few emoticons)

Again, learn your audience and respond accordingly. Blend like a chameleon.

Women are probably the worst at accepting compliments … about anything. They are the nurturers, accustomed to taking care of others before themselves. Often, they worry they're being selfish or boastful if they aren't humble enough in their responses.

If you do a good job, no matter your gender, be proud of your work, and thank those who compliment you on it. It truly makes people feel validated—on both sides of the conversation—when you do.

TIP 342: Overcoming procrastination

Okay, let me start by acknowledging that there is a big difference between taking the time to ponder an option to make an informed decision, and avoiding something through procrastination.

I am a productive person, as anyone who knows me will tell you. I'm never bored and I don't embrace idle time. That's just who I am. However, there are certain things I procrastinate about—cleaning my bathrooms, doing my taxes, and emptying the fridge, to name a few.

But when it comes to something I'm passionate about, I am the opposite of a procrastinator. I jump in with both feet and go full speed until something stops me.

However, I know that not everyone is of that mindset. Some people like to take their time to make decisions, and while I can respect that, opportunities tend to pass us by when we wait too long.

So…

Here are 11 ways to battle (true) procrastination:

1. Set a real deadline for a project and write it down. Simply saying you plan to do something is an idea. Writing it down and working toward it makes it a goal. Stick to it and get the work done. If you say you want to write 1000 words per day, do it. Otherwise, it's much like that disgusting toilet. As time passes, it will only get harder to tackle.

2. Change up your routine. If you are the type of person who is not easy to motivate every day, try getting dressed as if you are going out first thing in the morning, rather than lounging around in your PJs all day. Just because you "work at home" doesn't mean you have to look like homemade sin. I always feel better when I get up and brush my teeth and hair first thing, even before I eat breakfast. It may sound weird, but it gets me "in the mode" for productivity every day.

3. Instead of one large goal, break it down into several smaller goals. If you are a goal-oriented person like me, it will be satisfying and validating to check off even the smallest of tasks each day.

4. Enlist help and then stick to your deadlines. If you can get someone (preferably a spouse) to watch the kiddos and maybe handle dinner one evening, perhaps you will be more motivated and focused.

5. Prioritize your daily tasks. I personally choose to get my most-challenging or least-favorite tasks out of the way first. But if you'd rather do the more-enjoyable ones first, feel free.

6. Eliminate distraction. Learn what your distracting patterns are. Do you turn the TV on first thing in the morning? Check emails? Surf the Internet? Try doing that after your tasks (or at least a few of them) have been completed. Change your routine if it's not working.

7. Set a reward for reaching your goals or finishing mundane, dreaded tasks. But don't let it be something too distracting.

8. Have others keep you accountable if you must. Tell them about your big projects and ask them to help keep you on track.

9. Don't be a perfectionist. Many people procrastinate because they are afraid of "getting it wrong" or "not doing it well

enough" (to their standards). Sometimes you must let go of a little bit of that control and say, "Good enough is good enough." Of course, I'm not saying settle for sub-par efforts or results. But don't stress over it so much that it affects your health. You will always be harder on yourself than anyone else. Give yourself a break every now and then.

10. Learn to forgive yourself. You are not evil or selfish because you didn't make that deadline, reach that word count, or finish that certain task. You are human, and humans are not perfect. Give it your best effort and that will shine through in your results. If you are sick or stressed out, you will not produce good work.

11. Use apps that help you track your progress. There are even some that connect you with your friends to compare or share results.

> https://nozbe.com/?a=C68B1FD6
> http://www.goalsontrack.com/
> https://lifetick.com/
> http://www.stridesapp.com/
> http://habitlist.com/
> http://www.irunurun.com/

I must point out that if you are experiencing panic or true stress over a certain project or task, it may not be the right one for you, if it's affecting your health. Only you can decide that. Perhaps you need to get someone else to help or manage it for you? Perhaps you need to break it down into several weeks rather than hours or days?

Be realistic in your daily, weekly, monthly, and yearly goals. Don't stretch yourself more than you can handle, but do challenge yourself.

Having said this, many people (especially creatives) are much more efficient at working under stressful situations and even produce their best work during these times. Therefore, you must learn what works for you. Figure out why you are procrastinating and then construct a game plan to tackle it.

TIP 343: The company you keep...

I'm sure you've all heard the phrase, "Birds of a feather flock together." Well, it's true. My parents always told me to beware of who I choose to let in my life and spend time with, because their poisonous attitudes can seep into your soul without you realizing it.

I strive to be a positive, uplifting person. It turns out, being bullied throughout much of my adolescent life was a blessing in disguise. It taught me about the fragility of the human spirit and how kindness is the most important asset a person can possess. It will take you further in life than any amount of money or fame, and it will definitely take you further in the afterlife.

Of course, I have two great parents to thank for a large portion of who I became, but other "toxic" people played major roles in molding the person I am today.

The reason I'm including this topic in this segment is because writers (and artists in general) are among some of the most emotional beings on Earth. This can go in either direction, too. We can be extremely sensitive and timid about any kind of criticism or negativity, or we can be the strong, outspoken types who are always ready to defend what we feel is right. Either way, we are passionate beings.

So when a group of authors come together, the passion is almost tangible, because we are all so invested (in one way or another) in our love of language. We know the power that words hold.

But this can also cause hurt feelings if the outspoken ones think they are "helping" the timid ones by "giving them a dose of reality." That's often the reason many talented authors, who had the potential to go far, give up writing. They encounter toxic people either online, or in their personal lives.

Now, let me be very clear that there is a difference between critiquing and criticizing. Critiquing involves a spirit of wanting to encourage and uplift by instructing. Criticizing comes from a spirit of wanting to tear down others by discouraging and insulting them. See the difference?

Take what family members, friends, other authors, and even strangers say with a grain of salt. Just because you are polite enough to listen to their words doesn't mean you have to absorb them to your very being.

Authors grow with helpful feedback, honest feedback, but they must learn to discern between encouraging advice from those with more experience, and negative complaints from those who want to pull others down to their level.

Ultimately, don't take advice from someone who isn't where YOU want to be, personally or professionally. We choose to keep people in our lives for specific reasons – to teach us something (mentors), to make us work harder (inspirations), to lift us up when we need it (supporters), to tell us what we want to hear and offer us an escape from responsibility (enablers), to let us know when we're on the wrong path (regulators) … and then others are there to learn from us. Not all relationships are meant to last.

Let go of toxic relationships and be aware of the company you keep.

TIP 344: Finding your voice as a writer

This tip is about a topic that many authors struggle with, some for years, before they get it right. I'm talking about finding your authentic voice as a writer.

As a child care provider for many years, I've been privy to elaborate conversations between some of the most imaginative creatures on earth—preschool-aged children. When these youngsters step into the roles of Mommy, Daddy, or Baby, they do it without reserve, without fear. They don't worry about who is listening. In fact, they submerge themselves so deeply that if they happen to catch me watching them or listening in on their lives, the imagination becomes diluted. Perhaps they fear being judged or "getting it wrong." But until that point, they are the ultimate creatives, making it all up as they go along. It's believable, entertaining, and most of all … authentic. They become their characters.

Actors spend hours digging deep into their beings to find the voice of each specific character they portray on television or in movies. Each new role requires a new voice, a new personality.

Writers face the same challenge. Unless you are writing a series using the same characters repeatedly, you will need to find a new character's voice each time, so he/she comes across as authentic as possible.

When developing a new character, ask yourself these types of questions:

- How old is your character? You may have to step into the mind of a child, a character who is the opposite gender of you, or even a dark character who does things or says things you'd find unthinkable otherwise.

- What is this character's personality like – shy, bold and outspoken, crass, foul-mouthed?

- What level of education has this character received – in school and life in general? Meaning, did this character even finish high school? Was he/she raised out in the country with limited academic opportunities? (If so, he/she might have a somewhat-limited vocabulary and language skills. Think "Bubba" on the movie Forrest Gump.)

- What adjectives describe your character – physically, socially, and emotionally? Self-abusive, self-reliant, stubborn, angry, resentful, easy-going, etc.

- Close your eyes and step into this character's shoes. (This is what actors do as well.) Pretend to interact with the world (and people) around you. Stand up and act it out if need be. How does your character feel when in the presence of these people? Is he/she comfortable in the setting? Does he/she feel threatened?

- Read other books with a character who is similar in personality to the one you are creating. Learn his/her mood, tone, strengths, weaknesses, and little nuances in facial expressions or body language.

- Does writing/creating this character feel forced? Does the dialogue come easily and flow well, or does it read as boring or harsh? If YOU feel this way about it, chances are, your readers will as well.

- How would this character speak if addressing your ultimate reader (target audience), in his/her most comfortable style?

Imagine being that four-year-old acting out the princess scene.

• Read dialogue passages to others (who have an ear for great writing) and ask, "Does this character sound authentic to you?"

Characters can be created from personal experiences of the author, or they can be completely fabricated from imagination. An author can create a character who embodies the person he/she wishes to be—stronger, braver, more authoritative or assertive, sexier, more adventurous, sweeter, etc.

Finding your voice with each character is crucial to the success of your story, its ability to relate to your target readers. Asking yourself these types of questions can bring you one step closer to creating memorable characters that readers love to love, or love to hate.

One of my favorite quotes is:

"A reader lives a thousand lives before he dies. The man who never reads lives only one." George R.R. Martin

The same could be applied to authors, as we are the creators of these life-altering tales.

TIP 345: The write way to get through the holidays

Between family gatherings and shopping, one thing many authors struggle with is finding time to write during the holidays. Heck, there isn't much alone time to do anything during this hectic season, much less something that requires as much focus as writing.

Here are 9 ways to stay focused on your writing during the holidays:

1. It's all about time management. Just as you would set aside time to shop, bake goodies, or send Christmas cards, be sure to make time to write.

2. If you don't have a specific project to work on, write a short story or poem about the holidays, to get yourself into the spirit of the season.

3. Set small goals and reward yourself if you reach them. The holidays are a great time to find seasonal goodies like pies, cookies, and special candies.

4. Tell your loved ones you're going holiday shopping but really slip away to a Starbucks (or better yet, a library) for some writing time.

5. Get up early or stay up late. Dedicated writers rarely get enough sleep. They do what they must to fit writing time into their lives. It doesn't last forever, so do it while you can.

6. The holidays usually mean homes are brimming with extra people. See if you can get someone to watch the kids for an hour or two so you can knock out some writing. Teens or childless individuals are usually more than happy to hang out

with the little ones. Be respectful and stick to your deadline, so you can spend some time with the family too.

7.   Writing during the holidays requires more planning so be sure to plan your schedule out each day (even better, the day before) to make sure you can fit everything in. Go into it knowing that you will need to stay on task to get everything done and you won't be overwhelmed.

8.   Keep a notebook with you at all times. You may be struck with inspiration during a simple conversation. Perhaps a character profile will pop into your head while you're talking to your sister, or a plot twist will evolve from hearing her relationship woes. Jot it down – not in front of her, of course.

9.   Take care of yourself. Many people suffer from depression or other health problems because they are "so busy" and don't have time to eat right or rest properly. Don't deprive yourself of nourishment during this hectic time. You will need every ounce of energy you can muster to keep up with your schedule.

With all of that said, if you would rather take time off and enjoy your friends and family instead of write, that is a personal choice, and an admirable one. Don't feel guilty for doing that.

Writing can be like exercising. Once you get out of the routine, it may take a while to get back to where you want to be. The brain is a muscle that must be consistently worked. Set a date upon which you will get back to your writing, and then prepare to do the work.

Don't forget to enjoy the holidays with your friends and family. They only come once per year and you never know when it will be your last.

TIP 346: *Striking a balance*

This tip focuses on balancing your writing life with your personal life. We are all people. Therefore, we ALL have personal lives aside from our writing—whether this involves spending time with our four children or our forty cats. Or it could even mean a quiet night at home alone, sitting by the fireplace.

As writers, we can be "tortured" (in a good way at times) by our writing. It can keep us from sleeping, eating, or even showering when we'd prefer to. It can also (though many times unintentionally) alienate our loved ones. Authors can go from one extreme to the other in their writing careers—putting it off for months at a time to handle personal matters, and then diving back into it for months at a time, neglecting those around them. It becomes a vicious cycle of guilt and shame that can affect both our personal relationships as well as our professional reputations … and not always in a good way.

I am as guilty as any other author in this matter. It takes time and practice to learn how to balance everything, and it's an ever-changing process as life throws us curve balls. But I do what I can when I can, and that is all I can ask of myself. However, I have gotten better with each published book, learning from my past poor decisions. I've realized what my limitations are and how to capitalize on my strengths.

Here are 9 tips for balancing your writing life and personal obligations:

1. Learn to say "no" to some things. Don't take on extra beta reading, editing, or blurb-writing tasks IF you don't truly have time to devote to them. It doesn't do you or the friend you are

trying to help any good. Distractions can keep you from giving the project your best effort, and your relationship with those who want and need your attention may suffer.

2. Making an outline for your story and dividing it into sections is a great way to ensure you stay on track. This also allows you to skip around to work on whatever portion of the story you see fit at any given time, which eliminates the "writers block" or "getting stuck on one part" aspect of writing.

3. Get your household chores AND your writing done. This is not the same thing as multi-tasking because you will not be focusing on more than one task at a time. Since writing is actually my leisure activity, I "reward" myself with writing sessions. My house has to be cleaned up (eventually) because I have several people living here who need clean clothes and food once in a while (smile). Therefore, I will allow myself a set writing session time for each major task I complete. For instance, I won't sit down to write until I get the bathroom cleaned or at least two loads of laundry done (my two least-favorite chores). Not only does this break my cleaning up into segments, it allows me to go back to my writing each time with new ideas and fresh eyes.

4. Give your full attention to whatever task you are working on at any given time. If you have set aside some time to write, close the door and ask not to be disturbed. Set a timer so your loved ones know when they will be able to interact with you again, instead of giving the constant response, "Just one more minute, honey. I'm almost done."

5. On the same note, put your phone/computer/note pad away when you are with your loved ones. Let them know they have your undivided attention. Those emails and Twitter and Facebook notifications will still be there later.

6. Skip watching television or anything else unnecessary that can take the place of your writing time. If you are serious about writing, you don't have time to waste. With that said, don't give up things that relax you or give you a welcomed break. It's not healthy to plant yourself in front of the computer for hours on end with no food, sleep, or at the very least, a good stretch on occasion. Your eyes will grow tired and your muscles will become sore. This is based on your own standards. If you know you really want (and need) to be writing, turn the unnecessary distractions away. This includes connections on social media. Don't engage in them while writing unless you must.

7. Don't be afraid to delegate some things. Not as far as your writing but obligations around the house. If you have older children who are capable of doing chores, assign tasks for them each week to help maintain the home. You can still oversee the major tasks (i.e. cleaning out the fridge, filing the bills, etc.) if you're a control freak like me, but they are perfectly capable of helping out. Don't feel guilty to the point that you make yourself responsible for everything in the home to "make up" for lost time because of your writing.

8. If you have people in your home (writing environment) who deserve your attention, you aren't only ignoring them when you are writing. They also feel alienated when you are reading, engaging on social media, or even researching something online. Keep in mind, all these things still divert your attention away from them. Just because you aren't technically "writing" doesn't mean you aren't ignoring or neglecting those who matter. Creating memories is just as important as creating the next great story.

9. Make the most of your time. If you have a little one taking a nap each day between 1P.M. and 3 P.M., don't spend an hour of that time engaging on social media when you should be writing. Or, you can do that if your writing is caught up and

you need to network or focus on marketing your books for a while. This is also a great time to work on scheduling blog posts. Try to get a week's worth done at a time so you won't be stressing out at the last minute, scrounging for a blog topic.

10. Take care of yourself. Exercise, eat healthy, and do things that rejuvenate your body and spirit. You are no good to anyone if you are sick, exhausted, or cranky. Meditate, pray, take a long bath, or simply sit in your rocking chair on your back porch listening to the sounds of nature. As authors, our minds seem to always be "on." Sometimes we need to quiet the voices inside our heads (and around us) and simply be. You might be surprised how many plot twists, solutions to problems, or story endings can arise from these quiet, non-trying moments.

I've offered nine ways to keep your writing life and personal life in check. It's not easy and it doesn't happen overnight. But with practice and a bit of awareness, you too can live a fulfilled, balanced life as an author.

You can find these tips and more in my new video-blog segment on YouTube by clicking this link. Be sure to subscribe to my channel so you won't miss one!
https://www.youtube.com/channel/UCSa4YNcX4DOvqMQge Uhj_VA

TIP 347: 11 ways to find inspiration for your writing

Whether or not you believe in writer's block, as a writer you will most likely face a lack of inspiration at some point in your career.

Here are 11 ways to stay inspired in your writing and keep the words flowing:

1. Become a people watcher. Go to a park or a mall and sit, watching people interact with each other around you. Don't be stalkerish about it but watch their facial expressions, their body language, and listen to the tone in their voices. You can learn a lot. Then jot down a few paragraphs to describe those scenes. You may end up with a story idea.

2. Read, read, read. Choose stories that are in your specific genre. Pay attention to how the words flow and how the dialogue is set up, and how it affects your mood while reading it.

3. Join a critique/support group – book clubs are great for inspiration and bouncing ideas off one another.

4. Visit a local children's hospital and learn what they go through. Those kids are some of the most inspirational beings you'll ever meet. You'll gain a whole new appreciation for life and the words may flow like honey from there.

5. Check your short-term goals list. If you haven't looked at it in a while, you may be surprised to find that you've achieved a few of the goals you'd set. That can lift your spirits and perhaps get you back into the writing mode.

6. Enter writing competitions. Other than book sales or great reviews, nothing lifts an author's spirit faster than winning a

writing award. It makes all those sleepless nights and days of ignoring your loved ones worth it.

7. Talk to an author who is much higher on the success scale (what you consider successful) than you are. Listening to his/her backstory may inspire you to keep going with or pick back up with your writing. Or you can read the backstories of famous authors.

8. Help another author by mentoring him/her or reading his/her book and reviewing it. Seeing another author excel or be lifted up by something wonderful happening in his/her life can be quite inspiring and fulfilling.

9. Watch a movie or television show. Before you guys quote Stephen King on me about TV being a mind-destroying abyss, I don't mean binge watching mindless TV or movies. But I must admit sometimes it helps me come up with plot twists or character descriptions when I watch my favorite TV shows. Shonda Rhimes is my writing hero.

10. Go find a few inspirational quotes or memes and post them on your social media timelines. People will comment on them and some will even thank you for them. Reading those comments and seeing that there are people in the world needing what you are needing makes you feel connected somehow. That can be a huge inspiration and spiritually rejuvenating experience. Sometimes simply looking at beautiful scenery online or in person can make a huge difference.

11. Get organized. Sometimes all it takes for me to regain inspiration is to clean and organize my workspace. This applies to everything in my life. You know that feeling when your bedroom has become your laundry room and it looks like your closet threw up, because you've had a hectic week and dread cleaning it? But once you do clean it and put all the junk away, get rid of some clutter, and make everything pretty again

(reclaim your space), if you're like me, all you want to do for the rest of the day is plop down on your bed and soak up the "prettiness" of what you created.

Inspiration is found where you look for it. It can come from anywhere around you—from people-watching in the park to discovering a new favorite author in your genre. You simply have to open your mind, your eyes, and your ears to the stories that are being told around you, that no one has written down yet.

TIP 348: 21 items to have in your writing workspace

Every job that must be done in the world requires certain tools. Doctors need scalpels, stethoscopes, thermometers, etc. Bakers need flour, sugar, butter, etc. All these items are needed for these professionals to do their jobs.

Though the tools vary from author to author, their purpose in the writing process is the same—to aid in getting the job done right. And like doctors, lawyers, bakers, and other professionals, writers must prepare their workspaces to allow them to do the best job possible.

Here are 21 things writers might find useful in their writing workspaces. Some are used every time; others are only required on occasion. But they each serve a specific purpose when needed.

1. Pen or pencil – Many authors prefer to write their stories by hand, rather than typing them out. Some use a hybrid method. Even if you most often use a computer, it's still a good idea to keep a writing utensil handy. I personally prefer a pen, but a pencil will work in a pinch.

2. Paper/notebook – It makes sense that if pens and pencils are useful, paper will also be needed. There will be times when your creative process works better with pen and paper, especially when you can't get to your computer.

3. Post-Its – these are great to use in creating outlines, character profiles, and simply jotting down notes or plot twists.

4. Laptop or computer – At some point in your writing career, you will need a computing device, as opposed to solely using

pen and paper. You will need an email program, a word-processing program, and Internet for choosing images, sending emails and documents, and typing your manuscript.

5. Highlighters – These work great during editing because you are able to set apart certain text in a highly visible way.

6. Paper clips – You would rarely want to put staples or holes of any kind in a manuscript, especially one you might send to a publisher or editor. Paper clips are less obtrusive and less destructive.

7. File folders or some sort of filing system – These might be used for queries or rejection letters, or they may be used to store writing pieces for various projects.

8. A lamp or adequate lighting – This is very important for protecting your eyes, avoiding glares on the screen, and/or to allow you to see your words clearly.

9. A comfortable chair – You will want to invest (as soon as financially possible) in a quality writing chair, as you will be spending many consecutive hours in it.

10. A clean, spacious workspace – It would be ideal to have an actual desk, but almost any flat surface will work – a kitchen table, a dresser, or even a mobile desktop/laptop desk will suffice. You may find it easier to invest in a quality desk eventually, however.

11. Something that inspires you – perhaps a photo of your family, an inspirational quote, or even a serene painting.

12. Printer – There will be times when you'll want (or need) to print something—perhaps a manuscript or query, or even flyers for promotional purposes.

13. Foliage – Plants can provide a calming, serene effect as well as give off atmosphere-enhancing vibes or scents.

14. Recording device – in case you have an idea for a project while working on a different one. You may not have time to write it down or type it, but you can speak it into a memo quickly.

15. Bulletin board with push pins or dry erase board with markers – These are great for jotting down ideas during brainstorming or even making a note of an appointment of some kind.

16. Personal organizer/appointment book – No doubt at some point during your career, you will be scheduling events—Facebook takeover parties, book signings, etc. An appointment book will help you stay organized and allow you to plan your day, week, month, or year.

17. Headphones – These can be used to listen to background music while you write or edit. But sometimes, you need them to block the world out.

18. Favorite books – Many authors find it helpful and inspiring to be surrounded by their favorite books when writing.

19. Organizer cubes or trays – These can be used to hold several documents that need to stay in the foreground of your space, rather than being filed away. The cubes can be used to store office supplies such as tape, staples, etc.

20. Snacks – There will be days when you'll spend hours on end writing or editing and you will need energizing snacks. It's best to avoid messy food and drinks around computer equipment and other devices. Thermoses and bottles with lids are best for liquids. Chocolate is delicious, but it can make a mess on keyboards and even on your clothes because it melts so quickly. Nuts and pretzels are good options.

21. A clock – Especially if you are on a time limit, you will need to be able to keep track of time somehow while you write or edit. Even if you don't want to have a clock taunting you with the minutes, you can set some type of alarm to signal when your time is up or coming to a close.

These are not all necessities, but they are all great options.

Every writer is different. Some prefer to work in isolation, while others need to feel plugged into the world and they thrive on interaction. No matter how much or how little you invest in your workspace, make sure it's functional and practical for you. Professional writing is a business and should be treated as such.

TIP 349: Writing challenges or excuses?

Authors adopt the term "writer's block" as a reason they are unable to come up with new material for a blog, a book, song, or article. In my opinion, it's used as an "excuse" for not reaching goals.

People who make things happen do just that – MAKE things happen. They don't sit around and wait for success to come to them; they go after it with gusto. Chasing their dreams and goals is what gets them going in the morning, what drives them through their day, and what keeps them awake at night. Some people get excited about going to the gym, going to work, or getting on stage in front of a million fans. Writers get excited about creating stories, and touching lives with their words.

Those who have clear, definable goals have a plan in place to achieve those goals. They get up each morning and do "something" to help move them toward those goals. It could be writing short pieces, networking on social media to sell a few books, blogging to get their creative juices flowing, calling media outlets to set up book-signing events or interviews, reading a book to learn more about the craft, or even watching YouTube videos on formatting books for Kindle, etc.

One of my favorite quotes is:

"True authors are not just starving artists in the financial sense; they are always hungry in the lyrical sense. They write because they can't not write. They write to feed their souls and minds. But no matter how much they write, their hunger is insatiable; they always want more."

Here are a few common complaints (excuses) writers have, and some solutions (cures):

I don't have time to write.
We are all afforded twenty-four hours in a day. No one is allowed more time than the other. It's all in how we choose to spend those hours. Set aside special writing time – set a timer if you are limited on time. Turn off the television and take a break from social media.

I have nothing to write about.
Read similar books in your genre to get ideas and get the "itch" to write again. Like Stephen King says, "If you don't have time to read, you don't have time to write. Simple as that." I will take it a step further and say, "If you don't have time to read, you don't have THE TOOLS to write." Reading is studying for the big test—our books.

I'm not good at writing; I'm a terrible speller.
That's what editors are for, and great editors are worth every penny! A great editor can step inside your head and make your story shine in ways you can't imagine.

I don't like selling.
Unless you have the money to hire a publicist or you go through a traditional publisher, you'd better get used to selling. It's par for the course. Keep in mind, you aren't selling "your books." You are essentially selling yourself—your ideas, your passions, your emotions. Even traditionally published authors are being told they must maintain a certain level of social media presence and in-person appearances to sell their books.

I don't have the money to publish.
This aspect has more to do with marketing strategies and personal finances compared to the other ones, which deal with emotional and self-concept issues.

You must work within your budget, and it takes time to research to find ways to market your work without breaking the bank. One of the most cost-effective paths is connecting with fellow authors in online support groups and social media.

I'm just not feeling it; I'm too tired to write.
It happens—many times due to lack of sleep, nutrition, support from family, or time. I've already addressed the "time" issue. Eat healthy, energizing foods, get up and move around, or try writing a smaller piece, like a poem or short story, to get your creative juices flowing again.

I have no support system; I'm a single parent; I have no "opportunity" to write.
I get it. Time is one thing, but lack of support in your writing career can be a tough issue to manage. My kids constantly roll their eyes and I hear, "Oh, you're on the computer again?" even though I coach their soccer games, home school them, and have been home with them since birth—yeah, I'm a bad mom for doing something I want to do.

You have to find a healthy balance of your time. Don't ever ignore your family for your writing; the guilt may produce crappy books. Again, set timers to let your family know what times you will be writing (or reading). When that time is up, stop writing and go play with your kids. If you keep a schedule (and your promises), they will be more understanding about your writing.

I can't get much writing done because I'm constantly editing as I go.
You must find a way to stop doing this. Keep in mind that every author's first draft is garbage. It's the product of a bunch of ideas running around our heads that we put onto paper. It's called brainstorming for a reason—like a huge cyclone of ideas swirling around in our brains and we are pulling debris from that funnel to

see what we can make of it. Get your ideas down on paper. Create a beginning, middle, and end, and worry about the editing last.

I don't know how to use Twitter, Facebook, Instagram.
There is no rule saying you must use all of the social media platforms. Find a couple that work well for your schedule and writing styles, and then learn all you can about them. Research is part of every aspect of writing, even the marketing. Watch YouTube videos, read articles, or read books on this topic. Knowledge is power.

I'm afraid I will write something that's already been written. (plagiarism)
Newsflash: if you can think it, chances are, someone else has already thought of it. Perhaps they've written a book about it, or perhaps they weren't brave enough to write it. Either way, I've read a myriad of books with similar themes, characters, lines, etc. It doesn't mean I didn't enjoy them. The authors found a way to put their own touches in them. That's what matters.

I've shared ten writing challenges authors face and how to address them.

In my experience, there are three keys to great writing:

1. Learn from those who write better than you.

2. Write, write, write. I often say I don't write unless I'm inspired to. That's okay because it seems my brain is never "uninspired." I rarely sleep, and I keep a notebook with me because I get ideas at the most inopportune moments.

3. Research everything you can. The more you know, the further you go.

TIP 350: Facing your fears

Everyone is afraid of something, but one of the biggest fears nearly everyone has is: not being accepted by others.

This one fear is what drives millions of people to social media each day—posting snapshots of themselves in compromising situations or outfits, saying things they wouldn't normally say, posting and sharing things they don't truly agree with but they feel compelled to follow the crowd, like a flock of birds. "So many of my friends are doing it so I guess it's okay."

It's all a popularity contest of sorts. Who has the most friends, likes, shares, or comments can be compared to who got the most votes for student council or homecoming court. It's not always based on what you know; many times, it's a result of "who" you know in certain circles, and how much influence you have. Of course, it seems, as far as social media goes, the winners (the ones with the most likes and shares) are the ones who are the most controversial about subjects, or are willing to "bare all" – literally speaking, not metaphorically in this sense.

Seeing online popularity contests of this sort can leave writers and artists feeling as if nothing they can offer will be valued, and sadly this is (seemingly) proven true more times than not. A post about Kim Kardashian's latest relationship woe will garner thousands more hits than a thought-provoking one by a talented writer on any given day. It can be disheartening.

But that doesn't mean that what authors offer isn't of value. We simply have to be determined to find those who will value our input, our stories, our ideas. In doing so, we must face our fears---more particularly, our biggest fear—about not being liked.

It can be quite tempting to "join the bandwagon" and start posting ridiculous nonsense that in no way represents who we are as writers or even people in general. We can start to feel as if we need to post things that will make others "like" us, so we are accepted.

Personally, I've never been one to go with the crowd. I've been told I'm quite a likable person because I'm genuine. What you see—or read—from me is who I truly am. (Of course, this is the very thing that causes many people to not like me as well). I have always been and will always be more about quality and integrity than popularity or quantity. I make mistakes. I make poor choices, but they are mine. I don't blame others for my faults or misfortunes.

This may cost me income opportunities that would have been so easy to obtain, if only I'd followed the status-quo. But that's not me. I'm a leader, not a follower. And I'm always eager to share with others, things that have helped me on my journey, to save them the problems I faced.

How do I stay so positive and proactive and not get discouraged when things don't pan out the way I'd hoped?

I ask myself two things:
1. What did I learn from this experience?
2. How can I do it better next time?

My husband tells me all the time that his favorite thing about me is my refusal to settle. I wake up each day wanting to learn something new or do something better than I did it the last time.

That's how we grow as writers, as human beings. We learn from our past decisions and use those experiences to make better decisions as we move forward.

As well, the way I face my fear is by imagining the worst possible outcome. Okay, I published a book. In my mind the worst things that could happen to me are not: not having enough reviews, not selling enough books, or people not liking my work. No, my worst fear is: wasting or losing my gift of creativity. People will always be there to stand in my way; I know this from experience. People will always try to bash my ideas; I've learned this the hard way. People will always find something they don't like; it's human nature.

But you should never change who you are or what you believe for anyone else. You have your own ideas and creations inside, waiting to come out. You are your own worst enemy!

Now I'll address some other fears writers have:

I'm afraid I'll run out of things to say.
No matter how many times a week you see your friends, each time you get together, there's always something to talk about, right? Get acquainted with your mind, and then your pen or computer. There will always be something to talk about.

Everyone will hate my work.
No matter how big your marketing budget is, you will never reach everyone with your words. Take heart in that. Connect with those who do enjoy your writing. And get an editor if you start receiving poor reviews.

I'll never be as good as the famous authors of the world.
That's good news. Then you can be better. It all depends on how badly you want it, how hard you work, how much you learn, and how much you're willing to sacrifice to get there.

It's just too hard.
You're right. It's hard work, but if you want it badly enough, you'll do what it takes to succeed. Parenting is hard work. Marriage is hard work. But you don't give up on your kids or partners when things get tough. You bond, you learn, you cope, and you thrive.

I'm afraid I won't be able to handle the success.
As narcissistic as this sounds, this thought does surf through a lot of authors' minds. This part of the process requires a great deal of self-awareness, soul searching, and a loving support system to keep you grounded. Take one decision at a time, and involve the people it will affect.

I've shared with you all my biggest fears, and offered a few tips on how to deal with some other common fears authors have. Determine what is holding you back, address it, and move on. Your story is waiting to be told.

TIP 351: 7 great stretches for a writer

Sitting at a computer desk or a certain chair for hours on end can wreak havoc on your neck and back muscles. Doing so on a daily basis can cause headaches, backaches, neck cramps, and even leg cramps. That's why it's important to take breaks and stretch your muscles—all the muscles involved, even your fingers.

I personally have noticed a chronic pain in my right thumb and wrist. It's worse on certain days than others, but it's always there. I haven't gone to see a doctor about it yet, but due to my age, my family history, and my typing habits, I wouldn't be surprised to learn that it is a form of arthritis or carpel tunnel syndrome.

You guys probably already know I'm a huge fan of yoga for calming the mind and body. But there are also certain yoga stretches that can address pain and muscle tension.

Here are some basic stretches that may prevent, or alleviate, pain in your body while writing. Some of these may seem ridiculous at first, but they do help.

Eyes – Staring at a screen for prolonged periods of time can cause your eyes to become sore and dried out. You may even go several minutes without blinking and not realize it.
Try turning away from the screen for a few minutes, or hours if possible.
Close your eyes tight and open them again.
Then close them softly and open them.
Close them and roll them around slowly.
Slowly look down, up, and to each side.

If your eyes are dried out, apply Visine drops and let them rest for a while before returning to the screen.

If your eyes are tired or sore, apply warm teabags or cold cucumbers over them while closed and wait a while to return to the screen.

Fingers
Squeeze a stress ball.
Open and close your fingers tightly and release.
Bend one finger at time – fingertip pointing inward toward your palm.
Bend all your fingers backwards with your other hand.
Massage your palms with your thumbs.

Wrists – Massage your wrists with your alternating hands.
Roll your wrists in a clockwise and then counterclockwise motion, slowly.
Bend your hands at the wrists in alternating forward and backward motions. Shake your hands out at the wrists.

Neck – Stand and slowly roll your neck from the right, down to center, and up to the left.
Reverse that motion.
Drop your chin down toward your chest and hold it there for about ten to fifteen seconds.
Then hold it backwards for the same amount of time.
Stop when you feel pain, or slow your pace.
Massage your neck with your fingertips. This will help work your hands and neck at the same time.

Legs and feet – One thing I highly recommend for the legs is sitting on an exercise ball instead of a desk chair while typing. That way you can occasionally back up and bounce to keep blood flowing in your legs, which helps prevent cramps, spider veins, and tingling (legs going to sleep).

Stand up and slowly squat. Touch your fingertips to the floor as you lower and pull your chin down toward your chest.

Stand back up and lift one foot at a time behind your back, holding it toward your bottom for about ten seconds.

Get up and walk around.

Stairs are a great way to work your legs during writing breaks.

You can also lie on your stomach and pull one foot up at a time up toward your bottom with your same-side-of-the-body hand. (Example: pull your right foot up with your right hand). Turn your head in the opposite direction.

Point and flex your toes slowly. Rotate them in circles as you did your wrists. Massage the balls and arches of your feet with your thumbs if need be.

Shoulders and arms

Lift one shoulder up at a time toward your face.

Then do both shoulders.

Raise your right arm up in the air and fold it behind its same shoulder. Hold that arm's elbow with the opposite hand.

Switch and do the other one. Keep that position for about ten seconds each time. You can also pull your chin to your chest if you'd like.

Bring one arm at a time across your chest toward the opposite arm. Hold your elbow with the opposite hand.

Give yourself a tight hug.

Rotate both arms in circles, stretched out like a "T."

Raise them both above your head, like a "Y" and circle them around to allow your fingertips to touch your toes. Hold that position for about ten seconds.

Lower back and stomach

Sit up straight in your chair and twist your body to each side, only from the waist up. Let your feet face forward.

Get down on the floor on your knees and then "sit" on your knees, letting your bottom rest on the backs of your ankles.

Extend your hands straight out in front of you and lower your face to the floor. Sink into this amazing stretch at your own pace and hold it. The lower you go, the deeper the stretch.

Lie on your back with your arms out at a "T" shape. Use your left hand to cross your right knee over to the left side of the body and try to touch the right knee to the floor.

Go back to the original position and do the same with the other knee. Keep your arms on the floor as much as possible.

Do the butterfly: Sit on the floor and touch the bottoms of your feet together. Hold them with your hands and lower your head toward the floor space in front of your feet. Hold this stretch for about ten seconds.

Even if you don't try these, be sure to step away from your desk periodically and do some type of stretching or movement. Don't allow stiff muscles to cramp your writing style. (Pun totally intended!)

TIP 352: Tidbits of wisdom from experienced authors

If you study successful people long enough, you'll notice that many of them have certain things in common. No two people ever take the exact same path to fame, for sure, but I have learned that there are schedules and patterns (habits) involved.

According to the research I conducted on several famous authors, the following 14 habits were common among many of them:

1. Write every day.

2. Write with passion.

3. Read everything you can get your hands on.

4. Be consistent and patient.

5. Set goals and manage your time. Don't get sucked into social media. Develop thick skin for rejections, suggestions from beta readers, and reader reviews.

6. Don't procrastinate.

7. Have a marketing budget in place.

8. Edit without emotion. Don't get too attached to your words and don't be afraid to cut what needs to be cut.

9. Have a dedicated writing space.

10. Set boundaries for friends and family concerning your writing time.

11. Don't edit while you write. Write until the story is complete.

12. Don't share your work until the first draft is complete, because it may change.

13. Interact with readers/fans.

14. Form a good support team.

Those were all tips from well-known, traditionally published authors.

Just for fun, I decided to interview a few successful Indie authors as well for their #1 piece of advice.

Here are their words of wisdom:

Emma Scott – author of the City Lights series – see all of her books here:
Books by Emma Scott
"Make sure you release only your best work and have bloggers/readers who've already read it, ready to post their reviews upon release. Build those social media connections before releasing the book. Trying to do all of this AFTER your book has been released is like trying to put all of the eggs back together after the omelet has been made."

David M. Salkin – author of "The Team" series and several other suspenseful books. See all of his titles here:
Books by David M. Salkin
"Don't force it. Don't feel it today? Don't write. You can take days off… refresh… find something amazing… work when it comes back to you."

Kim Cox – author of The Lana Malloy series as well as other romantic suspense novels. Check out all of her books here:

Books by Kim Cox
"Learn the trade, read all you can in the genre you're writing, and also how-to books. Take criticism with a cool head and don't engage."

Mark Fine – author of "The Zebra Affaire" – an incredible book you can learn more about here, along with an anthology he was a part of:
Books by Mark Fine
"Being an author can be isolating. First task is to reach out to others via social media or local author groups, and then team up. Apportion tasks based on each team member's respective skill set, and then move forward as a collective. Collaboration is a powerful resource, and it should be applied in both a creative and enterprise sense. So team up, fellow scribes."

Laurence O'Bryan – author of Irish mystery novels and founder of the entity Books Go Social – check out his books here:
Books by Laurence O'Bryan
"Listen to criticism and modify your work where appropriate."

Karen Power – author of the Butterfly series – check them out here:
Butterfly books by Karen Power
"Treat your manuscript in the way a publishing house would, which means you should use an editor, professional typesetter, copy-editor, proofreader, cover designer, etc. Remember writing is a creative endeavor, and publishing is a business. Never short change your reader."

Gisela Hausmann – author of the "Naked" series – check out all of her books here:
Books by Gisela Hausmann
"Today so many people emphasize the importance of social media. I say, "Never underestimate traditional media! a) You can reuse it on your social media platforms to show your social media friends

that your work is relevant and noteworthy. b) If you do it often you will sell books. c) If you have been featured in traditional media a few times you will have an easier time getting speaking engagements."

Beem Weeks – author of historical fiction and sci-fi titles, and a contributor to an anthology that I have a few entries listed in as well. Check out his books here:

Books by Beem Weeks

"Always spend the extra money on a professional editor. Because even if you're capable as a writer, you are too close to the story. Editing is more than searching out typos and bad punctuation. Editors will see plot holes, redundancies, and portions that can and should be trimmed away to make the story tight and professional. That separate set of trained eyes will make all the difference in the world."

And just in case any of you would like to know what my one piece of advice is …

"Don't feel the need to compete with or belittle a fellow author to get to where you want to be. If you have something of value, share it with them. It's not a competition. It's the exact opposite. By helping others up the ladder, they will be there to give you a hand up when you need it."

Bonus resources to help you on your journey through authorship!

TIP 353: My 3 go-to books on writing

This tip is short, but important! I'm often asked what my go-to books about writing are. I've read a ton of books on how to write page-turning fiction, but three titles stood out to me more than any others.

Here are three books I highly recommend you have in your writer arsenal:

Harmony Kent – *Polish Your Prose*
Not only is she an amazing author, but she's an uber-talented editor who I've used for my own books.
https://www.amazon.com/Polish-Your-Prose-Essential-Editing-ebook/dp/B00OLVAYP0/ref=as_li_ss_tl?ie=UTF8&keywords=POLISH%20YOUR%20PROSE%20HARMONY%20KENT&qid=1462906412&ref_=sr_1_1&sr=8-1&linkCode=sl1&tag=awowitr-20&linkId=2cfa6a37dcc7d32fdbe50ab6540c9e47

Stephen Geez – *How-to Dialogue*
This author has traveled the world teaching creative writing and marketing for major corporations and individuals for many years. His book is an excellent resource on constructing dialogue for any writer—of fiction or nonfiction.
https://www.amazon.com/GeezWriter-How-Correctly-Compelling-Conversations-ebook/dp/B00DBBAGHC/ref=as_li_ss_tl?ie=UTF8&keywords=how%20to%20dialogue%20geezwriter&qid=1462905990&ref_=sr_1_1&sr=8-1&linkCode=sl1&tag=awowitr-20&linkId=22a148a9565bfb6b680f8b067910caeb

Carolyn V. Hamilton – *Power Editing for Fiction Writers*
This book is an excellent resource for writers who want to learn how to effectively edit their own books, and pack more punch into their writing.
https://www.amazon.com/Editing-Fiction-Writers-Carolyn-Hamilton-ebook/dp/B00ZYUM47I/ref=tmm_kin_swatch_0?_encoding=UTF8&qid=1462906564&sr=8-1

Now you know some of my writing secrets. I highly recommend these titles. They are loaded with tips to help you polish your writing, no matter the genre.

TIP 354: Writers' grants and where to find them

Did you know writers' grants exist? I didn't, until I stumbled upon a few of them in the past six months.

It's important to know that writers' grants are not simply free money given to just anyone to fund their writing/publishing endeavors. Applying for a grant takes time, research, and a great deal of effort and discernment; however, grants can be quite instrumental in an author's journey, especially since authors can receive multiple grants.

Most grants have themes or causes attached to them, such as supporting African American women in writing, or assisting emerging nonfiction authors who write about specific topics. Some grants are even state-specific. You need to do your research to make sure you choose (and apply for) the right grant for your needs.

Here is an excellent article about various types of grants offered to artists from all genres:
http://www.writersdigest.com/writing-articles/by-writing-goal/get-published-sell-my-work/free-money-for-writers

This grant is available once per year:
https://www.arts.gov/grants-individuals/creative-writing-fellowships

This is a website link for grants specifically created to support women:
http://www.womenarts.org/funding-resources/literary-indiv-artists/

Many celebrities and successful authors give back to the writing community by offering grants.

Here is a list of 19 grants, some provided by authors: http://www.freelancewritinggigs.com/2010/01/19-grants-for-writers-and-other-creative-types/

Another route an author can take to get funds for a writing project is to set up a Go Fund Me campaign. I've heard of several authors publishing their first books this way. Read more about this here: https://www.gofundme.com/tour/

As I mentioned before, be sure to take the time to research which grant is right for you. And don't be greedy. Be passionate about your project and thoughtful about your true needs and goals. With a little hard work and perseverance, you may be able to find funding for your next book!

Another one suggested by one of my blog followers: http://fundsforwriters.com/grants/

TIP 355: Protecting your work

When I first began publishing my books a couple years ago, I wanted to make sure that my words would be protected before I released them to the world. Thankfully, I have a friend who is a patent lawyer. He informed me that the fact that I am writing the words, and can prove they came from my computer is sufficient proof of ownership, and it would stand up in court. He also mentioned that ideas are not patentable. Products are. But, he taught me a little-known secret way to help ensure my writing doesn't get copied or stolen. He told me to add a copyright symbol to everything I write. Now, I put that little symbol on all my published works.

Here is how to make the copyright symbol: ©

Hold down the Alt key and then type in 0169

Also, in all my published books, I include this phrase on the copyright page, along with the © symbol:

All rights are reserved. No part of this book may be reproduced by any mechanical, photographic, or electronic process, or in the form of phonographic recording nor may it be stored in a retrieval system, transmitted, or otherwise be copied for public or private use—other than for "fair use" as brief quotations embodied in articles and reviews without prior written permission of the publisher.

The author's intent in providing this story is only to entertain. The characters and events are fictional.

Those two simple entries included in your works can save you a lot of grief. Just like you were taught in school—put your name on your paper ... but don't forget the copyright symbol, too!

Here is an add-on to this tip, by Stephen Geez:

Good advice, TMS. Many don't realize that once ideas are set in a tangible form, they are already copyrighted. The other two elements not required to own, but which could in a pinch be helpful, are informing others it is considered copyrighted (that symbol) or at the highest level registering it with the feds, which can be done in manuscript form or book form. The biggest advantages to the hassle and expense of the latter are that it's easier to establish a history and allows collection of treble damages in a legal dispute. Establishing the history is sometimes most important, as many cases of registering another's work have occurred. At Fresh Ink Group, any book with any kind of history identifies that on the copyright page, and when we put out new editions they are listed by date and version rather like software. We always document that history in our data file for each book, early drafts, alternate versions, partial material that appeared somewhere as a short story or excerpt, and so on. Think of it as digital paper in the advice a CEO gave me a long time ago when he said my people needed to document more: When the $*^&#%& hits the fan, whoever has the bigger pile of paper wins.

TIP 356: 15 Cool tools for authors

We all have those moments where we're sleeping or in the shower and a great plot twist or dialogue pops into our heads, but we forget what it was by the time we get to a place to write it down.

I've done this many times with songs, mostly because I do much of my singing and songwriting in the shower.

Well, fret no more, authors.

Here are some great tools that will enhance the writing/reading experience for you.

1. Writing in the shower or at night – Dive slate – reusable.

    https://www.amazon.com/Underwater-Writing-available-different-compass/dp/B005B1NVC2

    This glow-in-the-dark dive slate comes with a pencil attached and can go anywhere, and a Mr. Clean Magic Eraser will wipe it off easily.

2. Aqua notes – comes with 40 tear-off, waterproof sheets.

    https://www.amazon.com/Aqua-Notes-Waterproof-Notepad-Mountable/dp/B003W09LTQ/ref=sr_1_1?ie=UTF8&qid=1473163244&sr=8-1&keywords=aqua+notes

    Need to roll over in bed and jot something down? This pen even writes upside down!

https://www.amazon.com/gp/product/B000095K9D/ref=a
s_li_ss_tl?ie=UTF8&camp=1789&creative=390957&creative
ASIN=B000095K9D&linkCode=as2&tag=thwrli02-20

3. This is a great way to keep your book events, appointments, and even goals in one place that's easy to access, and it's completely customizable.

https://www.amazon.com/Planners-Magnetic-Refrigerator-
Calendar-
Horizontal/dp/B01D93US8I/ref=sr_1_1?ie=UTF8&qid=14
84337275&sr=8-
1&keywords=magnetic+dry+erase+calendars

4. Don't want to wake your spouse or kids up with the tap, tap, tapping of keyboard keys when a certain line of prose strikes you in your sleep? Perhaps this laser projection keyboard will solve that problem.

https://www.amazon.com/iNextStation-Bluetooth-
Projection-Ultra-Portable-Full-
Size/dp/B00WS3H3VQ/ref=sr_1_8?ie=UTF8&qid=147316
8745&sr=8-8&keywords=laser+projection+keyboard

5. Writers are usually avid readers. Reading for us is like studying for a test ... test meaning our published books. If you're a paperback reader, you might like these thumb-friendly page holders.

https://www.amazon.com/Thumb-Thing-Pageholder-
Bookmark-3-
assorted/dp/1578500486/ref=sr_1_2?ie=UTF8&qid=14731
68792&sr=8-2&keywords=thumb+thing

6. If you're an author like me who reads mostly on your tablet, but you don't always have your eyeglasses handy, perhaps this Kindle cover will solve that problem. With this kit, you simply

specify your prescription type and you receive the glasses and the handy holder band.

https://www.amazon.com/Reading-Glasses-Holder-Band-Tablet/dp/B0181X1Q6Y/ref=sr_1_5?ie=UTF8&qid=14731 66420&sr=8- 5&keywords=kindle+cover+with+holder+for+glasses

7.   Some writers print out their manuscripts and highlight the edits, so a clip like this would come in handy, rather than the writer having to flip pages. It holds up to thirty pages.

http://www.staples.com/3M-Copyholder-Monitor-Mount-Clip-30-Sheet-Capacity/product_562401?cid=PS:GooglePLAs:562401&ci_s rc=17588969&ci_sku=562401&KPID=562401&gclid=Cj0K EQjw0rm-BRCn85bm8uS-zK0BEiQAHo4vrK2omsF7tAqwA5vfo1YXkilfEG3JSrpG8 HGoIubXFlgaAgLq8P8HAQ

8.   This is perfect for reading during those luxurious bath times. I love that it has a secure wine holder. It even holds a tablet or smartphone!

https://www.amazon.com/UPGRADED-Bamboo-Premium-Luxury-Caddy/dp/B01D1S77MQ/ref=sr_1_8?ie=UTF8&qid=1473 166951&sr=8-8&keywords=bath+book+caddy

9.   And... to protect your tablet while in the tub, grab this waterproof Kindle cover. It fits almost any digital reading device.

https://www.amazon.com/Universal-Waterproof-Protective-Paperwhite-Keyboard/dp/B00KX8TY10/ref=sr_1_4?ie=UTF8&qid=1 473167098&sr=8- 4&keywords=waterproof+cover+for+kindle

10. And here is a waterproof cover for your phone.

    https://www.amazon.com/Waterproof-Case-Bag-Military-Lanyard/dp/B01G6XF0BI/ref=sr_1_4?ie=UTF8&qid=1473167352&sr=8-4&keywords=waterproof+cover+for+smartphone

11. These are perfect for reading or writing, when you just need to shut the noise of the world away ... without deleting the view. (Great for a mom/dad writer who needs to keep an eye on the kids.)

    https://www.amazon.com/Cancelling-Over-ear-Headphones-Saxhorn-Microphone/dp/B01G52IS5K/ref=sr_1_1?s=electronics&ie=UTF8&qid=1473169030&sr=1-1-spons&keywords=noise+cancelling+headphones&psc=1

12. Writers know how painful it can be to sit in a chair for hours on end to construct a patch of dialogue or figure out a story ending. This is a two-in-one back cushion, made of memory foam for ultimate comfort, and breathable mesh to keep you from sweating or sticking to your chair.

    https://www.amazon.com/Sweet-Relief-Support-Cushion-Adjustable/dp/B01AAZFMS4/ref=sr_1_1?ie=UTF8&qid=1473183287&sr=8-1&keywords=back+support+for+chairs

13. For the writer on the go, this laptop cooling station is perfect. The mouse pad on the side can also double as a writing station for those who need to jot down notes on paper.

    https://www.amazon.com/iMounTEK-Portable-Laptop-Table-Cooling/dp/B018WNXPEE/ref=sr_1_2?ie=UTF8&qid=1473168149&sr=8-2&keywords=portable+laptop+cooling+desk

14. I've saved the coolest of all for last. These sunglasses have a built-in MP3 player, allow hands-free calling and voice recording, and they have polarized (interchangeable) lenses that have the function of anti-rays, no glare and they promote good eye health care. These are perfect for those days when you want to read on your tablet or work on your laptop outside!

https://www.amazon.com/Bluetooth-Sunglasses-Handsfree-Headphones-Replaceable/dp/B00VJCFVWA/ref=sr_1_8?ie=UTF8&qid=1473170152&sr=8-8&keywords=mp3+bluetooth+sunglasses

There you have fifteen of the coolest tools that make the writing/reading process more convenient and comfortable. No more excuses not to finish that novel!

Side note:
Christmas is coming around again and these would make great gifts. I'm willing to send my mailing address to anyone who wants to buy any one of these for me. (smile)

TIP 357: HTML codes to enhance your Amazon listings

Have you ever looked at books on Amazon and noticed that some authors have enhanced descriptions and bios? (bold, italics, colored). Well, in this tip, I'm going to show you how to incorporate some simple font (html) codes to enhance your content, too.

Here are some basic codes you may encounter: (There are mixed fonts and formatting types used in this tip to teach coding.)

<!DOCTYPE html> – beginning of any document, but you won't need this (or the two below) for Createspace or KDP
<html>
<body>

<p> </p> – paragraph – signifies the beginning of a section of text

<b> </b> – bold text OR <strong></strong>

<i> </i> – italicized text OR <em></em>

<u> </u> – underlined text <u></u>

 – single line break

<font color="9900003> </font>

Now that you know what these codes look like, I will explain how they work. Basically, each line in a document has a code that tells

112

the browser what to display. If there are no codes, the browser will display a default font type, size, and color.

You will notice that each of the html codes above has a corresponding "end tag" or "closing tag" which tells the browser where to stop the insertion of that code.

**A simple way to think of this is: breaking down each part of the <code>

<b> – start bold font and </b> close bold font. The / stands for "close" as if closing a door.

Here is some sample coded text:

<p><em><strong><i>"Five stars have never made me feel like this. Where are my Kleenex?" Allaina Daniels</i></strong></em></p>

And this is what it translates to: (bold face font and italics)

"Five stars have never made me feel like this. Where are my Kleenex?" Allaina Daniels

If you only want certain words within a sentence in bold or italics, or you want to change the color of certain words, you can do so by adding the codes before and after those words.

<p>"Five stars have <strong>never</strong> made me feel <strong><font color="9900003>like this</font></strong>. Where are my Kleenex?" <i>AllainaDaniels</i></p>

"Five stars have never made me feel like this. Where are my Kleenex?" *Allaina Daniels*

Here is the code for italics only:

<p><i>A gripping story of love found, lost, and rediscovered in a magical way.</i></p>

And this is what it translates to:

A gripping story of love found, lost, and rediscovered in a magical way.

I am learning more each day, and with each book I publish, about html code. There are too many codes to list here, especially when you get into font size and family type, but these can help you garner a little more attention on Amazon.

This is what my one of my Amazon listings looks like using html code:
http://www.amazon.com/*Unsevered*-Traci-Sanders/dp/1517058244/ref=tmm_pap_swatch_0?_encoding=UTF8&qid=1454501627&sr=8-1

Here are a few links that will come in handy for beginners.

To check your html code as you go, you can visit: http://www.onlinehtmleditor.net/. This is a great FREE tool that you can use to make sure you added the correct codes.

For choosing a font color you can visit: http://www.w3schools.com/colors/colors_picker.asp.

The color you choose will be the 6-digit alpha/numeric code under the HEX column (ex: ffffff, ff0066). Do NOT add the # sign, only the code.

You can always contact my web designer with any questions you may have about coding. She's happy to help, and she's very reasonably priced.

Jennifer McDaniel
jenniferkmcd@live.com

TIP 358: What you can "write off" as an author (tax deductions)

Are you an Indie author? If so, you are a contractor, whether you like it or not. Regardless which company you publish with, you will be required to answer a few basic questions to set up your tax account with them. When you sell any books, they need to know how and where to send your money.

Therefore, no matter how much (or how little) money you make on your books, you must claim it, because the publishing companies do.

The good news is, you also have tax deductions available.

Here is a list of deductions you can claim as an author:
- Office supplies
- Telephone/internet fees
- Cabs, subways, bus fares
- Book, magazines, reference material
- Agents' commissions (if included in income)
- Film and processing – book trailer fees
- Copying – brochures, flyers for events
- Editorial fees – costs to hire professional editors
- Promotional fees – advertising materials
- Office rent – If you use a dedicated space for your writing – cannot claim for two businesses at once
- Utilities – a percentage for your writing (dedicated) space
- Memberships (professional organizations) – book club fees, writing organizations
- Messengers, private mail carriers, postage – shipping costs for giveaways, etc.

- Business insurance
- Tax preparation fees
- Travel costs – for out of town events – conferences, signings, etc.
- Business meals and entertainment
- Equipment – rentals of video/audio equipment for events
- Software – writing/editing/illustration software
- Legal and professional fees – patent lawyer, copyright lawyer
- I actually claim the books I buy and read because I consider them "study material" for my craft, especially those in my genre.
- As a public figure, for instance, when you do book signings and other events, you must have a professional appearance; therefore, you can write off your salon costs, new clothes, and even the food you serve at the event. Just be sure to keep the receipts and make notes on them.
- If you are at lunch and you pass out a business card or book to someone, write off that lunch by writing the person's name and the book you talked about at what became your "business luncheon."
- Treating your writing business like a professional entity will help you save money and avoid tax audits in the process, especially if you are like me and operate a separate business at the same time. The deductions must be kept separate.

Here are a couple add-ons to this tip, shared by Stephen Geez:

Research can be an important expense to track. That 250-word essay I'll be writing about what it's like to spend a month scuba diving in the Caymen Islands is definitely going to require some hands-on research…

Just thought of another point that used to be very useful: If you're writing for a client, an assignment, an intended buy, or even if you eventually sell to a client, you might be surprised by how much the end-user will be willing to reimburse expenses that s/he can write off. Don't leave that money unclaimed if a bit of assertiveness might compensate you. You could find that the combo of reimbursement and your own write-offs can cover 100% of the income.

TIP 359: 8 ways to save money
(that can be put toward publishing costs)

1. FOOD: Cook at home as often as possible. Plan a menu that includes every meal for the week and stick to your grocery list. Allow yourself to eat restaurant food only once per week—better yet, once per month. I have found that food cooked at home tastes fresher and is much healthier for your body because YOU control the sodium, sugar, and fat. Have a meal-prep day. Cut your vegetables and prepare sides ahead of time—perhaps on a Saturday or Sunday (for the entire week). Go ahead and set the meat out for that morning and let it be marinating for dinner that night. Then all you have to do is throw it on the grill or in the oven and cook when you are ready. Don't plan your meal for that week based on Buy-One-Get-One-Free specials at your local grocery store. Instead, plan it with whatever meals you'd like. Then, go purchase the Buy-One-Get-One-Free items to use in stocking your freezer or pantry—basically … overstock. You'd be surprised how quickly your stockpile grows. After a couple of months of doing this. You will realize that your grocery bill will shrink because you will have an ample supply of some items each week. And NEVER shop when you are hungry!

2. PLAN AND BUDGET FOR SPECIAL OCCASIONS: You know these things are going to come up every year–birthdays, anniversaries, and the big one … Christmas! Try to either set aside a "discretionary fund" for these expenses and add a little to it each month, or buy these items when you see them on sale and save them for the upcoming occasions. For instance, shopping for Christmas decorations, cards, and presents, immediately after Christmas can save you a significant amount

of money. The same goes with Halloween costumes. The stores need to get rid of the merchandise quickly to avoid returns and restocking.

3. UTILITIES: In winter, wash and dry clothes during the day to help warm the house. It will keep your thermostat at a steady temperature, which prevents the unit from having to work as hard. During summer, try to only do laundry after the sun goes down, and try to limit it to one to two loads per night. Ask your utility company to come do an "energy conservation" check in your home. They will check for any area that allows leaks of energy—such as windows, doors, etc., which can save you a significant amount of money in the long run on your utilities.

4. INDULGENCES: Love that special gourmet coffee from Starbucks, Dunkin Donuts, etc.? Now it is sold in retail stores like Kroger and Publix. If you are a huge coffee drinker and simply must have that "treat" every morning to function, make it at home—add whatever flavored creamer or whipped cream you like.

5. FUEL: Fill your car up on gas as often as possible, rather than putting in ten to twenty dollars' worth here and there. Kroger has a great incentive plan where you earn fuel points for spending a certain amount of money in their store. It's best to wait until the end of the month to fill up your tank because you get the biggest discount. Instead of ten cents per gallon savings, it can be a significant as sixty or seventy cents' savings per gallon!

6. SHOPPING: Shopping online for clothing, shoes, etc., can save you a significant amount of time—and fuel. Instead of standing in line at retailers, not to mention the stop-and-go effect on your fuel usage, and wear-and-tear on your car, you can buy many things with the touch of a button these days. And many companies give you added discounts and free

shipping! I highly recommend (ebates.com) https://www.ebates.com/r/TRACIS511?eeid=28187

7. They reimburse you between 2 percent and 7 percent on every purchase you make, for companies they are affiliated with.

8. CLOTHES: Sell some things you no longer wear or need on e-Bay or Amazon. My rule is, if you haven't used it or worn it in two seasons, you probably aren't going to. Give someone else a chance to benefit from it.

9. PAY YOURSELF: Every time you don't dine out at a restaurant, forego that gourmet coffee in a store, resist the new shoes you saw in the mall, or didn't buy that gorgeous bracelet from HSN; reward yourself by putting the money you would have spent on that item in a jar, or better yet, in an interest-earning account.

BONUS: Saving money is not a big thing—it's a lot of little things that add up. It's choices we make every moment of the day. To eat out or not, to use the stove or the grill, remembering to leave the water running just a little during the winter to keep the pipes from freezing up or not, to allow our kids to play several sports or simply focus on one at a time.

These spending habits boil down to—individual needs, personal preferences, and will power. When we choose NOT to go over budget, we are not depriving ourselves of things—we are empowering ourselves with financial security and peace of mind.

TIP 360: 5 items an author should always have handy

Since self-published authors are basically their own marketing specialists, they must always be ready to not only talk up their books to strangers, but also close sales with them. Most book sales are lost and long forgotten once the potential customer walks away. So it's best, if possible, to lock the reader in during the initial conversation.

New York Times Bestselling Author Louise Hay sold her books out of the trunk of her car when she started out. And her first book began as nothing more than a small pamphlet of information.

Authors should be willing to do what it takes to get their book into as many hands as possible, to reach their target audience. And readers are more likely to buy a book that they can pick up and feel in their hands, check out the cover, and flip through a few pages. They also are more likely to buy a book from "a person" rather than a site, if the person is friendly, genuine, and knowledgeable about his/her product.

**It's important to note that this is not always the case at book events, as many customers feel pressured by pushy authors, especially if meeting them for the first time. But if it's a one-on-one, organically-formed meeting in a social setting, the chances of a sale are higher.

So, in addition to knowing your story inside and out, there are a few things authors should always carry, wherever you go ... because you never know who you will meet.

- Business cards and/or teaser cards for your books. You could meet a cashier behind the counter of a restaurant while traveling, or even just a person who likes to read, sitting beside you on a plane or train. This person could end up being your #1 fan, and you never know who is in his/her circle of friends.

- Cash (as change) or a Square Reader to accept credit cards, in case someone wants a copy of your book. If you keep a few copies on hand in your vehicle, you have a better chance of making a sell right there on the spot, rather than the person taking the time to "go online later" and buy your book. The best laid intentions.

- A pen. Just in case someone wants to buy one of your books on hand, as they will definitely want to have it signed by you.

- A laptop or tablet. Just as you would take one with you to a signing, it's a good idea to have some type of digital device with you at all times. If someone wants to buy your book, while you are talking it up, you can go online right there and show them the reviews on Amazon or other sites, if they ask. (And bookmark your trailers/websites to locate them easily when necessary.)

- A notepad or digital-note-taking device. Ya know, in case a great story idea strikes.

As an author, you must always be ready to talk up your book, present your book, and make it as effortless as possible for interested parties to find/buy your book.

Bonus: I suppose we could add breath mints or gum to this list. You surely don't want to miss a sale because of your offensive coffee breath.

TIP 361: A writer's 3 best friends

This tip focuses on a topic that is not often mentioned in author circles – similar to the #1 rule about Fight Club: don't talk about Fight Club.

Well, I'm talking about it.

There are several resources available for writers to help hone their skills.

Even if authors don't like to admit they use reference materials to guide their writing skills, they do. If they don't, they should!

There are three resources I use as a writer practically every day. And unless you have learned everything there is to know about every word that exists in the world, you should take advantage of these tools as well.

1. **Dictionaries** are great for discovering the meanings, spelling, origins, pronunciations, and various forms (parts of speech) words can be used in. (Ex: Many words can serve as nouns and verbs.) Here are three to choose from:

    - Merriam Webster
    - Chambers
    - Cambridge

2. **Thesauruses** give us options by providing examples of synonyms and antonyms to use in the place of a certain word that doesn't quite fit in our writing pieces. I enjoy using a thesaurus to discover new words. I'm not ashamed to admit that I don't know the meaning of every big word I find in

books. But I research to make sure I'm using each one in proper context in my stories. I'm not the type of author to throw a lot of fancy verbiage into a novel to impress my readers with how "educated" I am. I keep things simple, and I think my readers appreciate that.

3. ***Chicago Manual of Style*** is like the bible for an author or editor. In fact, all the editors I've ever met use this as a guide. If you don't take advantage of this wonderful resource, you are missing out.

There you have it. The beans have been spilled. The cat is out of the bag. Okay, I'll stop with the idioms. Oh, are you not sure what an idiom is? Go look it up … in the dictionary.

Here is an add-on to this tip, shared by Stephen Geez:

Of these three, the only one I use is a dictionary, mainly for four purposes: to verify proper usage (is that also a transitive verb?), to confirm variations in spelling (fiancé vs fiancée, loath vs loathe), to learn about origins (not just of country and language, but also history of usage), and my big bugaboo: the right way to write a compound (based on what part of speech it's serving). For example, I'll wonder if sandcastle is a word, or if it's sand castle or sand-castle, or if hyphen is only when used as a modifier, and so on. My favorite dictionary is a Chambers. It's considered the world authority on English-language compounds, and instead of giving definitions in descending order of common usage, it gives them in historical order–whence came a word and how it was used over time leading to how it's used now. That information affects my choice of word and how I use the word (or phrase) more than one might think. Besides, I like understanding the words I use.

Traci's advice here is golden. My concern about Thesauruses is that too often writers use them as crutches–"Oh, THERE's a word for what I'm saying!"–without doing the REQUIRED subsequent look-up (see what I said above about dictionaries) to ensure the synonym or antonym found in a Thesaurus is the right choice and used correctly. When you start using words you've never heard, you don't have any cultural context. It's worth the effort to use a search engine and find a few examples of that word being used. That tree branch might be "gnarly," but having a 12-year-old use the word in dialogue is going to impart a different meaning than what a Thesaurus says. It only takes a few minutes to do this legwork, and I promise it will be worth it.

I nominate a good search engine to Traci's list, making it four sources. When I'm writing, I verify details as a matter of course, and when I'm editing someone else's work, that's a major part of the job. That WWII bomber built in the Netherlands? Sure, the guy who wrote this knows it's a Fokkur XXI. Well, no, it's a Fokker D.XXI.

This is excellent advice, Traci, to which I'll add: It's not enough to quickly check information about which you're unsure. THOROUGHLY check that information, and make the effort to routinely check even info you think you know.

TIP 362: And the award goes to...

The tips in this book series are being offered to help strengthen your writing and set it apart from others. One way to do this is to enter writing contests and awards programs.

Not only does "award-winning author/title" label sound good on your profile, the actual writing process involved in these types of competitions can force authors to produce only their best work. Writing contests often have specific themes, word limitations, and other guidelines in place to narrow down the entries. These boundaries give authors a sense of urgency, direction, and focus that is not always present in general writing tasks.

Writing competitions, especially ones that give feedback even to the non-winners, can serve as a motivator for authors to fix what was wrong with a particular story or their writing style in general.

Whether it's a small competition or a well-known award program, authors should enter at least two writing contests per year to learn how to write tight and adhere to deadlines. It's great writing practice, especially for those who wish to be traditionally published at some point in their career.

Here are some online writing contests that were being offered in 2016. Most of these sites tend to hold the same contests each year. Some require a fee. It's a good idea to choose ones that give feedback regardless of a win or not. You must do your research to find the right ones for your work. A few of these competitions even offer writing grants!

http://www.writersdigest.com/writers-digest-competitions/annual-writing-competition

http://www.newpages.com/classifieds/big-list-of-writing-contests

http://www.writermag.com/writing-resources/contests/

http://www.indiebookawards.com/

http://www.newpages.com/classifieds/writing-contests

http://www.pw.org/grants

http://www.freelancewriting.com/creative-writing-contests.php

http://www.freshinkgroup.com/contests/

Take your time, especially since many involve a submission fee, and choose the one that's right for you. Even if you place second or third, they typically offer a sticker or badge for your website or book to advertise your win.

TIP 363: The "I'm blocked' jar

As authors, other facets of our lives often play into our writing. Lawyers might write crime-fiction novels. Stay-home moms might write potty-training books or arts-and-crafts guides. A cardiologist might write a recipe book about heart-healthy foods.

As a mom and a child care provider for many years, I've had to be creative in finding ways to keep kids entertained and learning. Bored kids usually meant "kids who were ready to (or did) act out and get into trouble." So, I created the I'm bored jar.

I sat down with my kids and asked them for ideas of things they would like to do. We came up with one for each day of that summer and wrote the ideas down on small strips of paper. When we finished, we folded them into squares and stuck them in the jar. Each day of that summer, my kids took turns drawing a piece of paper from the jar and (weather permitting), that's what we did for that day. Even though we'd already done some of these things, and a few of them were simple – like building a fort—they never knew what was going to be on that paper. So, the anticipation was usually more exciting than the activity itself.

You can do the same as an author, to keep your writing skills sharp, to fill a blog segment, or to build onto a novel. Whatever the case may be, this one idea will ensure you write something every day, or at least every time you draw from the jar.

Let's call it the I'm blocked jar. Or the I don't know what to write jar. Regardless of what you call it, it can fuel your writing.

If you want to do a thirty-day challenge, come up with thirty writing prompts and place them in the jar. When I started this segment, I did this with my tips, and got as far as 150 in one day. Then I added more as I went along.

These don't have to be complete-sentence writing prompts. They can be short ideas (topics) you've always wanted to write about but wasn't ready, or wasn't confident you could.

Just as it was for my kids that summer, the element of surprise—not knowing what you will write about that day—can be an adrenaline rush.

So even if you can't get started with the writing today, start jotting down ideas of things you'd like to pen in the future. Add to your jar as needed. You never know what your mood will be like each day, and you may be inspired to write your best story yet.

Short pieces of writing include:
- poetry
- essays
- memoirs
- short stories
- flash fiction
- articles
- reviews
- journal entries
- children's books
- short plays – skits

You can even divide your novel into scenes, character sketches, etc., and write those on individual papers.

TIP 364: Sites that help hone your writing skills

This tip includes websites that can help authors sharpen their writing skills.

1. The first one is called One Word. The writer has only sixty seconds to craft the best story (well, paragraph really) possible based on one word. It's a lot of fun, and offers a bit of an adrenaline rush, to be honest. This is an effective tool that forces a writer to simply write, without editing or overthinking the words.

    Here is one I did recently, as an example: (for the word: bread)

    She stumbled down the stairs in her footed pajamas and rubbed her sleepy eyes. The scent of fresh-baked bread had lured her into the kitchen where she found her grandmother pulling a piping-hot pan of biscuits from the oven. She could almost taste the buttery flakiness as she took a seat at the table.

    Try it for yourself at:
    http://www.oneword.com/!

2. Another site I stumbled upon is called English Interactive. There are several exercises available on this site involving sentence structure, correct tense, grammatical errors, and much more!

    Check out the main site here:
    http://englishinteractive.net/writing/html

3. I also like https://owl.english.purdue.edu/exercises/. This one is good for brushing up on grammatical correctness, tense-change recognition, spelling practice, and more.

    Here is an example of a tense-change-recognition exercise: https://owl.english.purdue.edu/exercises/2/22/49/

With sites like these, and many others I didn't mention, available online today, there is no excuse for simple grammatical errors in professional writing. Try one of these sites or search the Web for others.

TIP 365: Use your voice

This tip is about a cool tool that comes in handy when you can't type (perhaps you're on a smartphone and don't want to use the keypad. Or maybe you're sick and don't have the energy to type, but you can talk.)

Regardless of the need, this Talk-to-Text program is a handy little tool for lots of things.

It's called TalkTyper, and it's fairly accurate, if you speak clearly and have a decent microphone available.

You can learn more about it, and use it by clicking this link. https://talktyper.com/

Another reputable one is Dragon NaturallySpeaking: http://www.nuance.com/dragon/index.htm

If you'd like to peruse all the options: http://www.capterra.com/speech-recognition-software/

Here are a few mobile dictation apps to choose from as well:

Dragon Dictation: https://itunes.apple.com/us/app/dragon-dictation/id341446764?mt=8

Evernote: https://play.google.com/store/apps/details?id=com.evernote

Voice Assistant:

https://itunes.apple.com/us/app/voice-assistant-just-use-your/id511757903?mt=8

Writers must maximize their time online and offline, so voice-to-text programs can be quite beneficial. Many programs are free, but if you plan to use the program often, and for important emails or writing pieces, it may be worth the cost of a professional version.

FINAL TIP:

The last piece of advice I wish to share with you all is this: get up every day and do ONE thing that moves you toward your ultimate goal in life.

If your dream is to be a full-time writer, you must do three things: Write. Publish. Promote.

These are ongoing tasks. They never stop!

Here is a list of things you can choose from any given day:

- research new sites on which to promote your books
- write a chapter
- write a character sketch
- learn to use Photoshop
- learn to use YouTube, Pinterest, Twitter, or Facebook to promote your work
- contact bloggers to schedule book tours
- contact media outlets to schedule interviews (radio, TV, newspapers)
- research and enter writing contests
- edit old manuscripts to improve your writing/editing skills
- network with fellow authors
- make promo images for marketing your books online
- take writing/editing courses
- create a budget for your marketing needs for the year
- create an email list and newsletter
- create hooks for each of your books
- talk to at least one new person about your writing (every day)

- brainstorm other ways to make money using your writing skills
- read a book to learn how to improve your writing skills

Break your big dreams up into smaller goals, and you may be surprised how quickly you gravitate toward them, and eventually reach them.

Persistence pays off. Never give up!

***

I hope you all enjoyed this book and learned some new things along the way.

Be sure to check out my upcoming titles, which contain the other tips that were offered in my segment.

Before You Publish: Tips on grammar, writing, and editing

Beyond The Book: Tips on publishing, marketing, and networking to build your brand

I also write parenting, children's, and romance titles. Feel free to check them out on my Amazon page here:
https://www.amazon.com/Traci-M.-Sanders/e/B00BA9VUUY/ref=sr_ntt_srch_lnk_4?qid=1486343706&sr=1-4

If you enjoy the books in this series, I'd be ever so grateful if you'd share your thoughts in the form of a review on Amazon, Goodreads, and any other social media sites you deem appropriate, to help other authors find them.

~Reviews keep authors writing!~

Special thanks to the following authors for their contributions to this book: (in no particular order)

- Stephen Geez
- Beem Weeks
- Emma Scott
- Gisela Hausmann
- Sharon K. Connell – beta reader
- Susan Kotch – beta reader
- Laurence O'Bryan
- David M. Salkin
- Mark Fine
- Kim Cox
- Allaina Daniels
- Karen Power
- Harmony Kent
- Carolyn V. Hamilton

Thanks to everyone who followed my blog segment in 2016, and for hanging with me in my video-blog segment for 2017.

Find me on YouTube:
https://www.youtube.com/channel/UCSa4YNcX4DOvqMQge Uhj_VA